# Change Your Mindset

*A guide with powerful strategies to master your thoughts, win your fears, change your habits and get success and in life.*

# Table of Contents

# Introduction

I had a difficult relationship with my father throughout my teenage years. I was perturbed about the fact that my father pushed me into depression by hurling out consistent criticism and abuse for no reason. I cannot say that I was an angel who was pure of every mistake, but the fact is that my father exceeded his limits at points. The results were disastrous for me. I felt low esteem and I couldn't concentrate on simple tasks. A time came when I had no confidence left. I wasn't sure whether I could do something about it or not. It was hard for me to finish simple things like fixing a light bulb into its holder and mending the fence that was broken by wild boars. I was disturbed about which turn my life was going to take. I remained in depression and had suicidal thoughts. I had been cursing the circumstances that I thought were responsible for my present condition. I was approaching my teenage years, pushing myself through the eye of a storm. It was a hard time.

Instead of ignoring everything around me, I took everything to heart and consequently had to bear the brunt. I failed in everything I tried because my brain just couldn't accept anything positive. It had learned to live and survive in dejection, and that took its toll on my career. I missed out on some of the most magical opportunities in my life. I failed in whatever I started because I lost consistency, perseverance, patience, and I must admit, the sprightliness of life.

By the time I hit 25, I had become a loser. I didn't have a career, any new opportunities, or a clear vision for what I wanted to do with my life. I thought I had made a serious mistake by reacting so passively and submissively to my father's atrocities. I confessed that it was a mistake to take everything to heart. Meanwhile, a friend of mine asked me to be patient and mend my ways to improve the quality of the years I have left. He said that it was never too late to start changing my mindset. Indeed, it was my mindset that was barring me from making progress, learning new things, and succeeding in life. I was only focused on the negative things in my life. Whenever I had to take on a new project, the first thought that popped into my mind was whether or not I would fail. I was a living mess. My negative thoughts found expression through my speech. This was a frightening time because the few friends I was left with decided to leave me; just like everyone else.

I decided to change myself. I read lots of books to help influence my mind. I banished negative thoughts out of my mind. I started feeling positive when I filled my heart with the desire to succeed in life. I set up goals and started working hard to achieve them. I must admit, the first few goals were hard to achieve, but gradually, I learned to be successful again. It was an uphill struggle against pessimism and negative thoughts, but it soon passed. When I changed my mindset, I was able to achieve the success levels that I never imagined I could achieve before. I reached the conclusion that everything existed in my mind. All my fears, doubts, and negativity existed in my mind and my mind alone. The biggest hurdle in my success was my mind. The source of all these problems was my mindset. Once I changed it, I was able to change the course of my life.

## What This Book Has to Offer

This book is for all the people who have had a similar episode in their life that I have detailed above. Throughout this book, you will learn different strategies to change your life. You will find out how your brain shapes your personality and influences your thinking. Here is a breakdown of the chapters of the book so that you may have a general overview of the contents of it.

- The first chapter of the book is the lengthiest because I think that a person's attitude is what determines how far a person will go in life. It is this attitude that helps people reform themselves and transform their lives. The first chapter starts with delineating the reasons for changing your mindset. I will explain different factors that are at play when a mindset is being formed. I will explain what vision is and how you can set a new vision for your life by replacing an old one. I will explain the importance of focusing on the present moment and how it impacts your life and how you can benefit from focusing on the present. I will also explain the methods of living in the present moment. The next section of the chapter carries details on the power of positive self-talk. You will learn how to turn your negative self-talk into positive self-talk in order to boost your productivity and get rid of the thoughts that drain your energy. I will go on to explain the importance of failure for success. What you can learn from failure and how you can turn it into success will also remain the subject of discussion. After this comes we'll talk about self-discipline, which has enormous importance with respect to succeeding in life. I will state some methods to enhance your discipline. We'll also further touch on the topic of sharpening your skills which are also an important part of our attitude. The section following this one will talk about how you can transform a boring work life into a fun and engaging one. You will learn to eliminate distractions that hinder your work. All of these subsections will be discussed in detail.

- The second chapter revolves around our habits. I will explain how you can upgrade your habits to boost your productivity levels. I will also mention a few rules to follow that will help to boost your productivity while you work. Some of the habits that will be discussed include optimization of the workspace environment, how to set goals, how to set up a daily routine, time management, etc. The chapter will end with a brief discussion about the fears we have in our lives and how they hinder our ability to change our mindset.

- The third chapter includes a detailed discussion on our fears. I will start the chapter off with a topic that defines emotions. Coupled with it is the topic of the types of emotions. After this, I will discuss the techniques by which you can master your emotions to change your mindset. Following this I will define fear, the causes of fear, and the reasons why fear can be your greatest asset in life. I will prove to you that in the absence of fear, we will not be able to succeed in life. The chapter ends with a discussion on how we can overcome our fears.

- The fourth and the second last chapter of the book focuses on how to live a happier life. I will explain how you can train your brain to be happy in all circumstances. Negativity can destroy you, but only if you let it. I will go on to explain how you can open your mind with the help of certain books. This section will dive deeper into the benefits of reading books and how you can transform your life with the help of books. The next section discusses details about the importance of improving your personality by consistently working on it. I will explain in greater detail why the cultivation of joy is important for you to survive in negative environments. I will also teach you the methods that you can use to cultivate joy and happiness. The chapter ends on the topic of the importance of taking care of your health and the benefits of meditation.

- The last chapter of the book helps explain how you can further improve on your changed mindset. You have become a positive person in your life but still, you have to work on yourself. You have to create a business mindset that will help you lead others. You will learn about the different personality traits of people who possess a growth mindset. I will also explain different ways to improve the business mindset. The next section of the chapter focuses on the mindset of a champion. I will explain how you can develop a champion mindset and how it can further help you succeed in life.

This book is for every age group, and for every person who thinks that his or her life is worthless. If you are facing dejection, negativity, pessimism, low self-esteem, and lack of confidence, this book will help you change your mindset. When you change your mindset, you will be able to conquer the world. You will realize that all those fears and doubts were just a figment of your imagination. Read on and soak up the positivity and happiness that bursts out of the contents of this book.

# Chapter 1: Improve Your Attitude

If you want to be truly successful in life, you should start doing rather than merely thinking. The first task you need to do is adopt a positive attitude. Once your heart is filled with the light of optimism and enthusiasm, you will see a dramatic rise in the opportunities you have and a significant fall in the number of problems in your life. Positivity is essential for people who love to lead others. Only a person who has a positive attitude can compel other people to take a specific action. This chapter includes details on why you should change your mindset, the importance of having a vision, the importance of self-discipline and focus, and the need for building upon your skills. With all this information, you will be able to bring about a positive change in your attitude.

# The Reasons to Change Your Mindset

Have you ever wondered what impact changing your mindset can have on your success and failure? What we believe can significantly affect what we achieve in life. What is a mindset? A mindset generally alludes to qualities such as your talent and the stock of intelligence you have. Some people have a fixed mindset and they believe that some qualities are inborn and they cannot be changed while others have a growth mindset, who believe that everyone can develop certain abilities through hard work and commitment. This notion can be explained by a simple example. Some children view every problem as a challenge that they must solve. They try to find something to learn from the experience. Other students view complex problems as impossible to solve. They get depressed thinking that their intelligence is being judged and scrutinized. The children who view challenges in a positive light have growth mindsets while the second group of children have fixed mindsets.

Our mindset plays a crucial role in shaping our personality and helps us cope with the daily challenges of life. If a student has a growth mindset, he or she will be able to bring about significant changes in their life when it comes to making an effort in job hunting or starting a new business. Also, people who have a growth mindset exhibit a higher level of resilience in the wake of failures. A growth mindset enables them to show perseverance when they are subjected to setbacks. On the contrary, people with fixed mindsets tend to give up easily.

One particularly bad habit of people with fixed mindsets is that they always need approval from others. In fact, they live to please others and that's why their biggest fear is rejection from society. They care a lot about how society will react to whatever they do. Will they be perceived as a winner or a loser? These thoughts play a significant role in putting a halt on their growth. On the contrary, people with growth mindsets have a hunger for learning. They believe that every experience they have is teaching them a valuable lesson. They also love challenges because they teach them something new.

### *Factors at Play on Forming a Mindset*

Generally, people across the world have two types of mindsets that are constructed by their experiences at home or at school. Let's explore how these two types come into existence.

- A child will have a fixed mindset if he or she is taught that he or she should look smart rather than seek learning. This leads them to focus on how other people are judging them. They are always fearful that they may not be able to live up to the expectations of those around them.
- A child will have a growth mindset if he or she is taught not to see mistakes as setbacks. They are encouraged by parents and teachers to try new things. They also learn from their mistakes and see this as an opportunity to build on their potential.

A growth mindset doesn't mean that a child starts thinking that he or she can conquer the world just as Einstein and Newton did. Instead, it means that he or she learns to live up to the maximum potential their life has to offer.

You can tell the type of mindset you have by studying your personality traits. For example, some people naturally are more intelligent than others. People are unable to change their basic abilities and personality traits. Some people think that talent cannot be acquired and what they naturally have cannot be changed. If you have thoughts like these, you have a fixed mindset.

On the other hand, some people have the power to change themselves. They believe that they can learn new things, and their intelligence has the capacity to grow and improve. In addition, they are not shy of working hard and acquiring and practicing new skills for the development of latent abilities. If you can think like this, you have a growth mindset.

*Why Change Your Mindset?*

Change is constant and it influences every decision we make and the path we take in our lives. Things are changing around us at a fast pace and we have to keep up in order to succeed in life. The business landscape is changing fast and new industries are jumping in. Technology is taking the world by storm by making its way into different fields. Change is an ideal path to happiness and success. I believe that our minds are powerful gadgets and by changing them, we can change the course of our lives. We can improve our lives if we can change the way we think and react to different experiences and thoughts. Our happiness depends on who we are and who we want to be. Here is a breakdown of the signs that indicate that you should change your mindset.

1. If you are constantly focusing on the wrong thing, you need to change your mindset. Sometimes, your mind fixates itself on disappointments and worries, and it just fails to see the positivity that comes your

way. I don't say bad things don't exist or they don't affect you at all, but there are high chances that a few aspects of your life remain in good shape. All you need to do is be thankful for the good things in your life because it will help keep the bad things out of your path. If you make it a habit of ignoring the good things in your life, there is a higher chance that you will not be able to use them to your advantage.

2. You are in a desperate need of changing your mindset if you happen to find yourself angry about suffering from a loss, and you don't believe in celebrating your victories. You always think that failure lurks behind each victory you have and that's why you cannot be grateful for life's precious moments even when you are succeeding. You cannot appreciate what you have achieved and this leads to frustration and dejection. This indicates a negative mindset and you need to change it. You need to realize that if you keep casting doubts on

your victories, you will remain ungrateful for what you have achieved.

3. A time may come in your life when you stop facing the truth. For example, the sky is overcast with clouds and it is raining on end for two days. You can curse all you want at the clouds and rain, but this won't make the sun come out. Complaints agitate your brain but do nothing else to change the situation. If you are not earning enough, you can change this by working harder; but there are some things that you simply cannot change such as the weather. You need to start accepting reality as it is to bring about a change in your mindset.

4. You need to change your mindset if you are always complaining about what you have in life versus what you don't have. Being ambitious is what everyone should strive for but too much of it blinds us to all the blessings in our lives that we already have. For example, if you want a luxurious bungalow your friend owns and a sports car

he drives while you live in a contemporary house and drive a Prius, you should not forget the time when you lived in a log house and you used to travel by bus. Striving for the best is something everyone wishes for but sometimes this lands us in a situation where we are never satisfied with what we have. This creates a vacuum that just cannot be filled.

5. If you like to play the victim role, your mindset needs a change. I am not saying that you are never wronged by people. There may come a time when you have been victimized by those close to you in some unfavorable circumstances. When you feel that you have been victimized, you should ask this one question to yourself: Does victimizing myself empower me? Be honest with yourself. Even if you have been victimized before, rejecting that role will help you take up a new and more positive role. Something that can surely empower you more.

6.  People always welcome dramatic endings and emotional scenes into their minds willingly. They welcome them so much that they go on to create some themselves at times. It has been evident over the past few years through research that people who have negative mindsets give space to alien thoughts that should not belong in their minds. These thoughts include messages from your parents convincing you that you are a failure and that you cannot pursue your dreams. The thoughts can be messages from your intimate partner who diminishes your worth as a romantic partner. You should immediately eliminate these scenarios and thoughts from your mind if you want to change your mindset. These thoughts are not yours. They are based on the thoughts of other people and reflect their judgments. Let go of them and clear your mind.

7.  Disagreements are a normal part of human interaction from time to time. However, if

you happen to be regularly disagreeing with people, it may indicate that you need a change of mindset. I am not talking about the people whom you meet on the street; I am talking about the people whom you trust and whom you respect in your life.

8. We don't always get what we want in life. This is just how the world operates. Your expectations remain unfulfilled sometimes and normal people realize this fact, but if you get angry and frustrated about unfulfilled expectations, you are not on the right track. If all your expectations are getting fulfilled, it is unnatural and unearthly. Expectations have a big impact on our minds. If we constantly set high expectations, we will never be satisfied with our life and this will lead to frustration and annoyance. For example, say you set a goal to be a billionaire by 45 but are nowhere near to reaching that goal. There is no doubt that you will feel frustrated. Some people are gifted with unusual skills and they

achieve this goal even before the target age they set, but not everyone can be like Elon Musk, the CEO of Tesla, who achieved everything so early in his life. Instead of building unrealistic expectations and increasing internal pressure, you should tune your mindset to think realistically and thrive in this world.

## Change Your Vision

A person's mission statement is a personal constitution for them that becomes the foundation for making life-changing decisions. It allows a person to adapt to changes in their life. If you want to succeed in life, you must create a personal mission statement to pursue, but it is also a fact that you cannot just write it overnight. It takes time. You have to answer several questions that come into your mind such as the 'why' factor in your life. Why are you doing something? You need to define the purpose of doing something. You must be clear about what you are going to do to change your life. Your vision is something personal and positive that drives you in your life and places you on the path to success. Having a clear vision in your life is imperative because it helps you stay focused and make conscious decisions about your priorities. A vision helps you eliminate distractions and helps you align the capabilities you have.

## How to Set a Vision in Your Life?

I was never convinced about setting a vision for my life but a friend insisted I create one. I found it silly and a sheer waste of time, but as I grew older, I knew I was wrong. Having a vision for your life is just as important as life itself. Without it, we cannot move an inch forward in life, let alone thrive. As I grew older, I realized that people abhor setting visions in their lives because they consider the exercise time-consuming, and even futile. People don't like setting a vision because they think it is impossible to achieve the goals they set for themselves. All the people who have accomplished something in their lives had a vision so concrete and clear that they see the oncoming days as if they were the future already.

People who get stuck in a web of hopelessness and chaos usually don't have a vision for their life. They pass time as if life is a burden to them. They hardly experience any moments of joy and there is no charm in their life. If you want to lead a great life, you must build a vision that will guide you. Goals are individual experiences that you must strive for.

Your life goals are something individual and personal to you. They are something you should strive for all the time. A vision is a bit bigger than that as it encompasses different goals you have in life. Your vision defines who you want to be and how you want to achieve something in your life. It defines the principles you want to base your life on. Your vision gives you a framework for the evaluation of these goals. It helps you know the answers to questions such as "what kind of life do I want to live in every new decade of my life?" It helps you decide upon the kind of people that you want to surround you along the way. It will help you believe in what you are capable of. It helps you understand what things you can accomplish under the right circumstances and motivations. A vision instills in your heart the desire to change something in this world to bring about something good.

If you want to create a vision in your life, you first need to identify key matters in your life. You must delve deeper into the details to know how you should live your life. You need to create a list of different categories that matter to you such as health which would encompass diet, perspective, and exercise. Let's create one as an example for you to understand what we mean.

- Health: I will consume a nutritious diet, practice regular and ample exercise, and practice mindfulness.
- Time: I will use my time wisely.
- Wealth: I want to be a millionaire by 30.
- Ability: I want to develop technical skills to excel in the job market.

This is a general list that you can agree or disagree with as per your priorities. It all depends on what you want to achieve in life. Some people give importance to lots of wealth because they don't have it. Others are born with a silver spoon and they value happiness and contentment over wealth. That's why their vision revolves around creating conditions that will guide them to achieve happiness. Some people are hungry to make a name for themselves. These types of people set lofty goals such as winning a world championship for running sprints, become a best-selling author, or make your name known in showbiz.

Whatever your objective is, you need to write down what you want from your life and think about something that you want to accomplish. You must work backward to decipher how a particular category you have included in your vision can support the same. A perfect vision must have a mission statement, which must be crafted in a way that describes in clear words what you want your ideal life to look like. This might seem a bit tricky as our priorities change with time, but you must have a general vision of how you would like for it to appear. A mission statement is not something that you should craft in a rush. Take your time. You can take a day off from work and craft it while you are away on vacation. However, make sure you are not having intrusive thoughts while you are creating it. Introspect until you get an answer from your inner self. If you do this exercise regularly, you are likely to see some amazing benefits in the days ahead. Your vision will stick in your head and compel you to work unendingly towards your goals.

## Focus on the Moment

The present moment is where we exist. There is no shortage of people who are in the habit of underestimating the present moment, but the fact remains that whatever we accomplish or lose in the present moment will be a part of our legacy.

What does living in the present moment mean when we are literally living in the present moment? It implies that we must be aware of each and every situation in which we live. It is about finding eternity in the moments we have. Usually, people have a bad habit of overlooking the mountain of opportunities they have standing before them. The exciting thing about the present is that it is ephemeral and it will be no more in a second. Our intense thoughts circling around a bumpy past and a little known future cause the present to slip out of our hands.

### How to Live in the Present Moment?

One of the best outcomes of simplifying our lives is to start living in the present moment and making the most out of it. Living in the present moment demands that we no longer worry about what happened in the past and how it had happened. In addition, we should stop worrying about what the future has in store for us. You should enjoy what you have today and live it to the fullest. Living in the past or in the future is detrimental to your mental health as it robs you of the excitement that the present brings you. When you are thinking more about the past and the future rather than the present, each day seems to be melting into next.

Forgetting the moments you have lived is not easy because we sometimes have possessions that remind us of the past; those possessions are what keep old memories fresh. These possessions may be photographs or household articles. The best way to get rid of past memories is to get rid of the possessions that are connected to them. Removing these possessions from your home means you are willing to let go of the past. Once the past loses power over you, you are more ready to live in the present moment.

Each day brings you a new set of hours that are full of possibilities. If you start your day with a smile, you are well on your way to cash in on those possibilities because you remain optimistic about your day. The most important thing is to be cognizant of what you are doing during the day. Coupled with this, practice the habit of appreciating the present moment. Try to soak up all the moments the present day offers you. Feel the sights, the emotions, the smells, the sorrows, and the sounds of the present day.

Everyone in this world carries at least one wound from someone in the past, especially a loved one. If you keep this wound in your memory, you are not going to live a peaceful life. The right way to live a peaceful life is to stop harboring any kind of resentment toward other people. The best way to do this is to forgive them and leave the past memories behind. If you allow them to affect your mood today, you are playing in the hands of your thoughts. You become a prisoner to your thoughts.

Many people complain about never being happy with their work. They always try to run away from what is happening in their workstation. They are always waiting for the weekend to start so that they can relax and remove the burden that they have accumulated throughout the week. The best way to eliminate any negativity from your work is to hunt down a new job which you can enjoy all the days of the week. I said earlier that you must not think about the future but this doesn't mean that you should not have any goals about your future. You have to think and dream big, and set your plans accordingly, but it's not enough to imagine what you want your future to look like. Pair it up with actions that lead you to the materialization of your dreams. You must take care that your dreams for the future are not adversely affecting the present moment.

A lot of people are in the habit of recalling how much success they've had in the past. How they lived in those moments and how they enjoyed them always remain in their minds. If you are talking about yesterday, you will not be able to cherish what you have today. As a result, you will not have more memories from the present to cherish in the future. One important thing is to stop worrying about what is going to come tomorrow. You cannot appreciate the present if you are thinking about what is waiting for you in the future. You need to realize that what has to come, will come anyway. The energy you are spending on worrying about the future can be channelized toward working out plans to materialize your dreams (Becker, n.d).

# Positive Self-Talk

Almost all people suffer from a mental condition in which a dialogue keeps spinning inside their heads. Sometimes, I have a song that runs in my head all day long. Some other things that circle around in my head are thoughts about an unfinished task or an incomplete piece of conversation with someone else. Your self-talk can be a random conversation about something you have observed in the environment.

Self-talk is usually done with yourself. There is no second person with whom you are talking to. You play the role of the speaker and the listener. If anyone says that they don't talk to themselves, they are lying. It is entirely possible, however, that he or she is unaware that they are talking to themselves. Self-talk leaves a considerable impression on our personality and attitude.

Self-talk is made up of the beliefs we hold and the biases that find a permanent place in our minds. There are positive and negative types of self-talk. It is your inclination towards a specific type of self-talk that decides how prepared you are to take on the challenges of life. Self-talk is not a problem by itself. The real problem is that we are generally hard-wired to remember negative experiences more precisely than positive experiences. We tend to forget what we have achieved in our lives and recall more often when we have messed things up, and this becomes a serious problem while we are on our way to shaping our mindset.

### The Power of Positive Self-Talk

Positive self-talk is not about being a narcissist but seeing things through a clear and realistic lens. Positive self-talk focuses on showing how much self-compassion you have for yourself. It is more so an understanding of who you are and what circumstances you have been through.

Positive self-talk is important due to the fact that it helps people overcome their body dysmorphia and performance, depression and anxiety, and low self-esteem. Positive self-talk can really make a great difference when it comes to fighting off pessimism and negativity. Positive self-talk has the immense power of beating down stress. If you are in the habit of practicing positive self-talk, you will be able to cope with stressful elements a lot easier than someone who practices negative self-talk. You will also be able to better fight off stressful situations as well as challenges in your life. This helps boost your confidence in whatever you are doing and boosts your rate of success. Essentially, positive self-talk transforms the way you view stressful situations. The more you practice positive self-talk, the more you will be able to approach the challenges of life in a more efficient manner and with a 'can-do' attitude.

Positive self-talk can help you polish your self-confidence in the wake of difficult situations such as building a business from the bottom up, excelling at the job you have, doubling your profits in your production business, mastering the skills you are studying at your university, setting goals and achieving them head-on, and recovering quickly from an accident or a broken relationship. It gives you the confidence you need to achieve whatever you imagine for your life. It helps you develop an attitude that helps you solve various problems of life when they arise.

You have probably met a few people already who you would describe as really positive and who are always working towards the goals they've set for themselves. They have magical levels of self-assurance and contentment. They are fully satisfied with what they have in their lives because they know that they can achieve whatever they want. Positive self-talk gives them immense confidence that allows them to tackle difficult situations with bravery and confidence. If you are hearing about positive self-talk for the first time, you might have difficulty in visualizing what positive self-talk is and how to practice it effectively. Positive self-talk involves repeating positive statements and phrases and have them looping through your mind. They help to boost your levels of confidence and happiness. Everyone has a different type of self-talk and everyone's strategy for self-talk is also different. Let's take a look at some examples that will explain what self-talk is and how it should be done.

1. I am proud of myself for pulling off this incredible and tough task.
2. I have enough confidence to change my circumstances. Eventually, I will transform my life.
3. I am working hard to bring about the much-needed changes that I have always sought-after.
4. I have the ability to be stronger in the face of adversity and negativity.
5. My failures have taught me great lessons to learn from.
6. Even though I have failed in life, I will never stop trying new things.
7. I have the ability to succeed in life.
8. Each new day is an opportunity for me to learn new skills and change my financial state.
9. I am proud of how much I have achieved.

10. I cannot control what other people think about me but I can change what I think of myself.

11. No matter how tough the circumstances will get, I will never give up.

12. I will take every challenge I experience in life as something that elevates me higher in the world.

13. I have improved upon my personality over the last few years.

14. I am a much better and more mature person than I was five years ago.

15. Each day offers me an opportunity to try again what I couldn't fulfill yesterday. I must get to work now to materialize what I couldn't before.

16. I will put all my effort into achieving what I have always dreamt of.

17. I will invest in myself by reading lots of books from successful entrepreneurs.

18. I will start the business I have always wanted to and I will succeed in the face of unfavorable circumstances.

## *Ways to Practice Positive Self-Talk*

Self-talk is not only about talking to yourself through your thoughts but it is about talking to yourself out loud. Positive self-talk is something that affects you positively in your life. You can tell if it is positive self-talk if the messages that are looping in your mind are motivating you and encouraging you to do something meaningful in your life. Let's look at an example. There are times in our life when we want to take on a new personality. I am the kind of person who likes to keep quiet and remain busy in my work. One day, I decided I wanted to try and be someone new. I decided to come out of my shell of quietness, so I decided to hang out with some friends at the beach. I tried to crack some jokes in front of my friends to make them laugh, but unfortunately, my jokes didn't go the way I planned them to. I couldn't understand if my jokes were bad or my friends weren't expecting to see this side of me. When I was on my way home, I had two ways to react to the situation. One was to curse at myself for behaving in such an awkward manner and the other was to tell myself that it was not a big deal. It's clear that the first thought is an example of negative self-talk while the second is a form of positive self-talk.

Put yourself in a similar situation. If you keep putting yourself down for behaving in an awkward manner, you will never stop questioning yourself whenever you are with your friends, let alone strangers. You will think twice before every sentence you speak, and this will perturb you. You will not be able to speak up on matters you are knowledgeable about because you are too worried about embarrassing yourself. You will feel bad about yourself and this will ultimately affect your confidence levels. It is highly likely that you will develop an aversion to any social event, as you may feel insecure about your interactions. This is very bad for your confidence.

On the other hand, if you convince yourself that you have done your best and you are proud of yourself, you will likely want to try again next time. The more you give yourself the chance to practice interacting with others socially, the better you will become, and as a result, the higher you confidence levels will rise. Each social interaction will help you learn something and improve something in your life. Self-talk is often overlooked by many people but it is so important; it shapes us into who we are and determines who we want to be and who we will be in the end. The things we tell ourselves determine the level of success that we will have. They also have the tendency to push us back into our safe shell and keep us paralyzed out of fear. Here is a breakdown of the ways through which we can practice positive self-talk.

- The first method is to harbor something higher than ourselves. People who have lofty purposes such as serving others, a higher level of spirituality, an inclination toward religion, or faith in social service, tend to have high self-esteem and a positive attitude. They have the power to turn their negative thoughts into positive ones. People who have pure religious sentiments such as a belief in the greatness of God, believe that God is kind and loving, and it is this belief that shapes their thoughts and the dialogues that run in their heads. These types of people are usually full of positivity.

- Another important thing to consider in order to achieve positivity in your life is to do away with people who are always negative. People are different and so are their attitudes. The problem with this world is that it is full of people who love to view experiences, people, and other things in a negative light. If you keep the company of these people, they will fill your heart with negativity. Surround yourself with people who maintain a positive attitude towards life, and you will be well on your way to living a life full of positivity. However, there are some people from whom you cannot distance yourself such as your family. The best way to deal with these kinds of people is to put a limit on the minutes you spend with them. If you notice a conversation going south, step away from the situation so that you don't get roped into a negative environment.

- One of the biggest hurdles in practicing positive self-talk is that our brain is naturally hard-wired to think about others and compare our lives to others. This is the bone of contention that needs to be located and driven out of our brains. We must stop thinking about the achievements of others or we will only hurt ourselves more. Everyone is born with a different set of challenges and blessings. If one person is born with a silver spoon or excels in mathematics or science, it is their natural domain that allows them to be this way. You cannot enter their domain and be a master player, but you can look into what you have got and work hard to excel in it. If your friends excel in mathematics, you might excel in fine arts or literature. All you need to do is find your domain and work hard to attain the level of mastery you have always craved. The comparison game destroys the dreams of many people because they get involved in things they are not created for. You don't know what others are going through. It is entirely possible that a student who was born with a silver spoon is not so well-off in the present moment because their father has accumulated a lot of debt and will soon go bankrupt. As a result, your friend will have to work hard to make ends meet, and for that, they will have to learn some new skills. As for the student who is good at mathematics and with whom you are comparing yourself, they may not be able to earn money in the same manner as you, an expert in literature or painting; you may be more successful in monetary terms than they will ever be. You never know what tomorrow brings for you so don't waste your today on negative self-talk about what you friend has that you don't. Remain positive and speak positive words.

- Fear of failure is something most people are afraid of. In fact, fear of failure kills more dreams than failure itself does. Killing this fear is the first step toward success in life. All great people who succeeded in life failed innumerable times before they achieved success. Your self-talk must not give room to fear of failure. Always think about how you will succeed in life and how you will conquer the world instead of thinking about what happens if you fail to deliver. If you give room to fear in your self-talk, you will not be able to break the status-quo and change your life. Failure is a compulsion. No one in this world is perfect, that's why they are bound to make mistakes and fail sometimes. It is how we treat failure that matters.

## Learn to Fail Before You Succeed

Every one of us dreams of achieving immense success in the world, in the financial realm, and the world of relationships. Have we ever dreamt of failure? Have we ever considered how important of a role failure plays in our success? Most people overlook the presence of failure in their lives. They discard the memory of failure as something nightmarish. This kind of behavior is somehow justified due to the fact that failure is connected to some dark memories that we want to get rid of at all costs. However we think about failure and how we treat it in our lives is one thing, and how it affects our lives and how it shapes our success is another thing. Whatever theories we have about failure, one thing is certain; that failure is inevitable. All of us fail at one point or another, regardless of the position we have or the situation we are in. Failure can be as simple as failing in the 1st grade or as big as failing in the presidential election of the United States. Failure can be as small as failing in running a small crockery store in a village in India or it can be as big as failing in entrepreneurial ventures just like the Indian business tycoon Vijay Malia, who was declared a proclaimed offender by an Indian court in a 9,000 Indian Rupees loan default case ("The Importance of Failure: 5 Valuable Lessons from Failing," n.d).

Let's accept the fact that we hate failure, but without it, success seems bland. There is no joy in something that comes to us without difficulty. We cherish the things that we achieve only after the effort and hard work we put into it. Let's take a look at the rundown of the reasons why failure is important in our life.

- There are just a few people who are born with immense strength in their arms and unlimited courage in their bosom. A greater chunk of people is inherently weak. They fear a lot of things such as failing in what they love. For example, my friend wanted to start a business in fashion, but he feared that he would fail. He feared that he wouldn't be able to attract enough customers to his shop. What if he couldn't afford to pay the rent of the shop? The grip of the fear of failure was so strong that he couldn't even take the first step. One day, he made up his mind to start anyway. He did and he failed to secure decent sales in the first few months. He had built up enough courage and understanding that he tried once more and invested what he had left. He succeeded in putting the business on a smooth track. It doesn't matter how many times he failed before he had been successful, but what matters is the conviction and the strength he had achieved from each failure. Failure tears us apart only to strengthen us. If you take the time to read the stories of the greatest personalities in the world, you will realize that all of them achieved success after making a considerable effort. Take the example of Elon Musk. He didn't succeed in producing electric cars overnight. After multiple failures in producing a battery set that would power the vehicle, finally, he succeeded in making a realistic set that could be installed in the cars. He had to inject the loan that was awarded to him by the US government for his space projects into his company Tesla to save it from bankruptcy. Now, he is in a position to proudly say that he has left behind failures to achieve robust success. We no longer see any unexpected ups and downs in the stock prices of the companies that Musk owns. It doesn't mean that he doesn't fail anymore, but it means that failure cannot break him down ("The Importance of Failure: 5 Valuable Lessons from Failing," n.d).

- Failure offers us an experience to seek guidance from for our future ventures. Failure is not something that is hurtful. It is how we choose to take failure which makes it harmful for us. Failure means that we had the courage to take on a challenge and we actually followed through it. We experienced a valuable lesson about what went wrong in our attempt to make it a success. That experience is of great worth because it has taught us a lesson, and it will guide us in our future ventures. Experience transforms our lives and improves our future-selves.

- Failure gives us a sense of direction where we must lead ourselves. Most people second-guess all the decisions they make. It is always appreciated if you double-check something before you bring it in the practical phase. Failure shows us how to place ourselves on the right track if we happen to swerve into the wrong one ("The Importance of Failure: 5 Valuable Lessons from Failing," n.d).

- Failure helps us grow as human beings. It helps us understand deep meanings about what we should do and why we should continue doing what we are setting out to do. Failure makes us realize how tough it is to achieve a goal that appeared to be smooth sailing a moment ago.

- In order to succeed in life, you need to be able to build a powerful level of resilience in your life. Your level of resilience will depend on the quantity of failure. Each time we fail, we become resilient to more failures in life. Each failure prepares us for a bigger failure.

It is this resilience that plays a role in our successes. It breeds success and helps us achieve our goals ("The Importance of Failure: 5 Valuable Lessons from Failing," n.d).

***Powerful Ways to Turn Failure Into Success***

In general life, failure has considerable importance, but it certainly is an important part of our business. It is a fact that we fail to acknowledge it, but we cannot ignore its existence. Generally, when we fail, we feel embarrassed. We go into hiding from family and friends because we want others to forget about our failures. We don't want it to be discussed openly and that's what makes us vulnerable to failure. We are ashamed of ourselves and we feel humiliated (as if we have committed some huge sin). This mindset needs to change. We must not let ourselves think that failure is a bad thing. We must think that failure is something that we must not be ashamed of. Instead, we should view failure as something that is of great value in our life.

The very first step toward realizing the importance of failure is to make yourself believe that mistakes are an inseparable part of life. If you are not convinced, you should read Paradise Lost by John Milton who explains how a mistake by Adam and Eve led to their fall from the heavens, and how they repented to regain what they had lost. Adam and Eve were ordered not to get close to one specific tree in a vast garden. They had all the blessings from God to enjoy their life to the fullest, but they failed in abiding by the directions they were given. Eve fell prey to the cunning tactics of Satan, who entered Heaven in the disguise of a serpent. Both Adam and Eve were led to believe that God had done great injustice to them by keeping them away from the fruit of that tree. Adam and Eve had a powerful urge to taste the fruit of that tree. They picked an apple from that tree and tasted it. Consequently, they were banished from the heavens. So, mistakes are not something to be ashamed of. There is always room to rectify what we did wrong (Khan, 2017).

We must be ready to identify our mistakes and learn from them quickly. If Adam and Eve didn't learn from their mistakes, it would've been an even bigger problem. They learned that whatever they do on Earth must be permissible by God, and whatever is not permissible, is illegal. Adam's repentance and acceptance of the rule made him the first messenger of God for the world. We must be ready to identify our mistakes to learn valuable lessons (Khan, 2017).

You need to be careful about how you are talking to yourself because, even if you're unaware of it, your subconscious is always aware of how you speak to yourself. Self-talk, after a failure, can be detrimental to your mental health. You must handle it well and mustn't allow it make you feel low about yourself. Do not let failure have power over your mind.

In order to turn failure into success, you must prepare a list of the reasons that led you to failure in the first place. Everyone has a list full of dreams and ambitions. You want to see your dreams fulfilled on your way to success. When you fail in materializing those dreams, you must lookout for the reasons that are behind your failure. Note them down and bring them into the form of a list to refer back to when you are trying to achieve the same goal in the future. This saves from repeating the same mistakes in the future (Khan, 2017).

I had a friend who was crazy about passing a civil services exam to win an administrative post in the public sector. He failed in his first attempt and instead of blaming his casual attitude, he blamed the system by saying it robbed him of becoming a civil service officer. He said that there was a lack of transparency in the marking of papers that led to his failure as someone else had cheated by tracing the papers and getting them marked at will. His blame was based on a hypothetical situation and was intended to suppress the sense of guilt that he didn't work hard enough to achieve his goal. When he had blamed the system and convinced everyone that the system was responsible for his failure, he went on to attempt the exam for a second time. This time, the results were no different. He tried a third time and got the same results. Thankfully, the third attempt was his last and he saved himself from becoming a laughing stock for the fourth time. The lesson you can learn from his experience is that he deceived himself by overlooking the reasons behind his failure. Instead of rectifying what went wrong, he went for face-saving, and that blinded him to the reasons that caused his failure. If you ignore the reasons for failure, you will not be able to change your future. Instead of overlooking them, you should be ready to learn from your mistakes. My friend overlooked the fact that he was not reading the right books while preparing for the exam. Someone asked him to consult guide books instead of doing his own research; and this is exactly where the problem was. He admitted this fact when he failed for the third time, but it was already too late. He should have learned this fact after the first time he failed. Also, his negative attitude didn't allow room for positive encouragement from his close friends. They knew that what he was claiming was wrong, but they kept silent because he was focused on placing the blame on other reasons (Khan, 2017).

## Enhancing Your Self-Discipline

Let's be honest with ourselves. Self-discipline, for most of us, is a work in progress. People who have a higher degree of self-control, tend to consume a lesser amount of time pondering on what behavior is deleterious to their health. This helps them make positive decisions quickly and easily. These people are less inclined toward getting affected by feelings or sudden impulses. As a result, they feel more satisfied with their lives. You too can build up self-discipline and attain a higher level of willpower to live a fulfilling life. If you are looking to have greater control over your habits and how you make choices about important matters in your life, you need to learn how to develop self-discipline.

Everyone, at some point in their lives, will make bad decisions that lead them to some form of failure in life. There are different excuses that can justify why we failed, but apart from all the reasons, lack of self-discipline is an important thing to take into consideration. If you are fond of reading books and consulting the encyclopedia, this knowledge is bound to go to waste if you lack self-discipline, because you won't be able to implement that knowledge in your life.

Self-discipline is having the power to do what you need to do no matter if your own feelings are aligned with it or not or if the circumstances are favorable or not. This is one ingredient that defines the level of your success and the durability of that success. You can only ensure constant success by being consistent in your struggles, and consistency is something that you can attain with the help of self-discipline.

### *Methods to Master Self-Discipline*

There are some concrete methods that you can adopt to attain self-discipline in your life. Here is a breakdown of those methods so that you can practice them and be able to bring about a significant change in your life.

- All of us have our weaknesses. We are easily distracted by things like Facebook, Instagram, Twitter, snacks, and a Marvel blockbuster movie. Whatever is affecting us significantly, we need to acknowledge its effects on us. The problem is, people don't like to show vulnerability and instead cover up any pitfalls they have experienced in their lives. The only way to fix this is to own up to their weaknesses if they want to overcome them.

- Willpower is also very important when it comes to building self-discipline in our lives. Willpower is what makes us different from animals. Willpower can be simply defined as a restraint on ourselves and an ability to resist temptation in all circumstances. It helps us identify the difference between what is right and what is wrong. For example, you are extremely tired and you don't feel like working but you have a project to deliver by the morning, and if you don't work overnight, you will not be able to deliver it. In this kind of circumstance, your willpower helps you gain energy to work through the night. You might be tempted by sleep but your willpower will resist any kind of temptation that keeps you away from your desk (Patel, 2019).

- The key to managing your self-discipline is keeping temptations in check. If junk food is a temptation of yours, you must stay away from all junk food if you have decided to lead a healthier life. Similarly, another temptation is social media; almost as bad as junk food. People nowadays are in the habit of constantly being on their phones, even during work hours. If this is something you recognize in yourself, you need to change this habit immediately because this decreases your productivity levels and shifts your focus from your goals over to useless things.

- People who have mastered the art of self-discipline, have one thing in common, and that is setting up clear goals in life. You must keep a crystal clear vision of what you want in your life if you want to maintain self-discipline because a vision is something that helps you stay on track. Setting up clear goals such as becoming a millionaire by 30 helps you understand the meaning of success to you. You must know which direction your are heading in because if you don't, you will lose sight of your target and you will be sidelined by others. A clear vision of your goals doesn't mean that you need to know what the final destination is, but it also means that your mind should be clear about the steps that you must take to materialize your dreams and find success (Patel, 2019).

- Self-discipline is something that you must learn along the way. It is a skill that you must master in order to lead a prosperous life. To excel in it, you need to make it a part of your daily practice. Self-discipline requires you to put in a lot of work, sweat, effort, and focus before you can implement it in your life.

- It is always a good idea to have a backup plan. You can call it "implementation intention." This technique is necessary to invigorate willpower. A backup plan ensures that you are ready at all costs in case a potentially difficult situation arises. If you have made a plan to build a business from nothing, you must keep some hard cash in hand to fend yourself from dry spells that usually come up in every business during the development phase.

- You must give yourself something to be excited about, such as a reward when you have achieved a goal or goals. Can you recall a time when you were a young kid and received a basket full of chocolates and candies because you had secured the first position in a school spelling bee? Did you feel motivated by the reward? Did you do well in the next contest? When you anticipate something good in exchange for fulfilling a task, you have a reason to put in your best effort to achieve that goal. Keep it going! When you have achieved something, you are well on your way to moving on to achieve something more in your life. Coupled with this is the tendency to forgive yourself if you happen to fail in life. Most people make it a habit to lash out at themselves when they do not achieve something, such as passing an exam or building a business. There is no good in doing that. You cannot move forward if you keep punishing yourself for past failures. The point here is to learn to forgive yourself and move on to face the next challenges once you have analyzed what went wrong (Patel, 2019).

## Sharpening Your Skills

Being a professional, there comes a time in your life when you are convinced that the skills you have acquired are not sufficient for succeeding in life.

The skills that are needed to get a job done change with time, sometimes so fast that it catches working professionals off-guard. For example, a few years back, it was enough to have one skill to earn a handsome amount to live a luxurious life, but since then, things have changed, and rather quickly. The demand for skills is changing. Website development was one of the top skills to acquire a couple of years ago but now it has been replaced by machine learning. Do you feel like the skills you have need a change because you no longer feel like you are in demand by employers? Even if you are satisfied that your skills are in demand, ask yourself this question: Are they enough to help make your life luxurious? Who doesn't want to make their dreams a reality?

### Surefire Ways to Sharpen Your Skills

Here is a breakdown of some surefire ways that will help you sharpen your general and professional skills.

1. Experience: Gain considerable experience so that you know how to do things in the

right way. Just energy and passion mean nothing in a professional environment. Experience gives you confidence in accomplishing a task fast and efficiently (Maxwell, 2014).

2. Ask for feedback: You need feedback for what you have accomplished to rectify your mistakes for your future ventures. Feedback sheds light on what went wrong and what could be improved upon. For example, if you are a software developer, you can ask for general feedback from your competitors on what they believe is working and what isn't. You can take into consideration their feedback as a reference for the development of similar software in the future. This is how you can develop your skills.

3. Online courses: You can take online courses to develop your skills. For example, for website developers, there are plenty of online courses for any new computer language that comes in the market. For example, Python has really become famous

among developers because of its multi-purpose uses. An online course on Python will equip you with the latest skills that you need to shine in the job market. Online courses also offer flexibility in terms of time and dates. You'll be sure to find a course that fits your needs and availability.

4. Professional certification: You can earn an online certificate for any skill related to the knowledge economy you feel you have expertise in. If you are a Search Engine Optimization (SEO) expert, you can get a certification from Google or any other competent forum to add to your skillset. Certification can make you more competent and credible in the eyes of employers. You can go on to expand your professional network with a certification in hand as you will be considered more reliable and professional by your colleagues.

5. The most important skill to excel in life is to go after opportunities rather than waiting for them to come to you. Remember the rule

that those who float in the middle of the sea waiting for help drown in a matter of seconds, but those who seek help will find some. Having the ambition to excel in life is one thing and striving to achieve it is another thing. To be called the best, you have to be the best. If you cannot stand out in a particular field, you will not earn more than your competitors. You have to do something that others are not doing like acquiring a new degree or demonstrating a new skill in front of your boss. You have to show others what you have to make them believe that you are the best of the best.

## Focus on What You Are Working On

You are so focused on completing a task in lightning-fast speed when suddenly something slows you down and you miss the deadline for your work. The delay may range from a few minutes to a few hours before you get back to work. When you eventually get back into it, you don't have the faintest idea about what you were doing and what was the last thing you were working on. If you can relate to the above lines, you are not alone in this. A majority of people suffer from the same problem.

This doesn't end here. The time you lose during that break is one thing, but the amount of focus that you lose altogether is what slashes your productivity levels. The momentum that you had built up and the level of creativity that you had achieved were all gone in a matter of minutes. The world is full of people who like to waste time and kill their productivity with their own hands. If you want to be like anyone, be like Elon Musk, who had such a brilliant level of focus that he used to block out the world while he read books. Remaining focused is about locating the right technique, realizing your priorities and then sticking to them without letting anything distract you. Let's take a look at some ideas for improving your focus.

### Have Fun With What You're Doing

Whatever you do in your life demands a huge amount of focus on your part. The best way to start anything is to ask yourself what is the need behind doing anything. By asking yourself this question, you will be able to locate the hidden desire for doing that work. For example, if you are a website developer and you have been hired to build a website, the probable answer is that you will get money and experience by doing the work. Also, you will be able to get more work if you do it right. Now, think of how you can make this task fun. For example, you can fuel it with creativity in design and content. Fire up your imagination to think about ways to make the website attractive and user-friendly. Think about your ideas and then find out how you can implement them to make the website look snazzy.

### Do Away With Distractions

Sometimes, your workstation can make you feel distracted because it is not neatly organized. If papers are spread all over the desk, your laptop is covered in dust and blots of coffee, and there is a complex web of wires hanging loose from the computer table, you will not be able to concentrate on your work. By nature, we love neatly structured things. If our workstation is messy, our brain will keep thinking about how to clean everything instead of focusing on our work. Until someone lands in our office and cleans our desks for us, we will remain distracted. Instead of drinking coffee at the desk and signing papers at the same table, you should find some other place where you can sign your papers and drink your morning coffee. This will help you deal with the distraction that deviates you from focusing on your work. People who have to work on their computers all day long also have to deal with other distractions that pertain to the computer itself. Things like keeping tabs open on your Internet browser to websites like Facebook and Instagram. In addition, we keep open an array of files at a time, which makes it hard to locate anything on our computers like folders. The solution to avoid these distractions is to cram all your files and folders in a single hard disk drive partition and if possible, a single folder.

### Grab Hold of Some Eatables

You must grab hold of some eatables like crackers or chips so that you do not rush to the kitchen to eat something when you start to feel hungry. Also, get some water to keep yourself hydrated during work hours. Remember that all kinds of rumbling in the stomach doesn't indicate that you are feeling hungry. You can do away with the rumblings by consuming a glass of fresh water. Sometimes, if you are not actually hungry yet you eat something that fills up your stomach, it may make you feel dizzy and induces sleep. That's why many people are found snoozing at their desks. This also derails them from being productive at work.

# Chapter 2: Improving Your Habits

Our habits shape our lives in a number of ways. Habits have a powerful yet somewhat shrouded impact on our lives because our brain tend to cling to them in all circumstances. Habits are not only important to make progress in life, but they also tend to grow stronger as we grow older. With the passage of time, we become more automatic. Our habits take control of our decisions, daily routines, and behaviors to an extent. This chapter carries details on what habits are, how you can improve upon your habits to be more productive in life, how you can set goals, and how you can set up a daily routine to achieve your goals.

## How to Upgrade Your Habits

It is often said that our habits are the only hurdle between what we are and what we want to achieve in our life. What we do from morning to evening makes up our daily routine. Improving your life is something you want to work on continuously, and it boils down to the smallest things that you do every day. What we call decisions are not actually decisions, but rather, they are habits that we are prone to do every day.

You may think that changing or upgrading a habit is easy, but in reality, it is a tough task to accomplish. Upgrading your habits is not as smooth sailing as we might think. In fact, it may turn out to be one of the toughest battles to fight. You know that you can have a better life if you change your habits but the problem is that upgrading your habits is a hard nut to crack.

The best way to upgrade your habits is to be productive during the day. This means that you should have enough time in the morning to break down your daily tasks into tiny steps, then scheduling your day from dawn till dusk. It is a good idea to create a schedule from morning to evening and then tweaking it throughout the day in case there is a better way of doing something. This schedule should entail everything you plan to do from the moment you wake up until the moment you lay your head to rest at night. You might think that creating this routine consumes more time than necessary, but it actually increases productivity. You are using your time and energy on something that will have an impact on your life and not on what outfit you plan to wear or what you plan to have for breakfast. Take a look at how much time you spend on deciding whether or not you have to go out for a walk or whether or not you need to put on a full face of makeup. Combine these short windows of time and see how many hours they make up, and take note of how much time you are wasting each day. Now, just imagine if you start spending this time on innovating something new or transforming something old.

A bedtime routine is something that you desperately need in order to upgrade your habits for success. If you want to have a healthy and incredible start to the morning, you need a perfect bedtime routine. If you have one, polish it to make it efficient. If you don't have one, you should make one and then follow the same. I have a routine which includes washing my hands, face, and feet before I dine with my parents. Before I go to sleep, I meditate in order to feel relaxed and calm my mind after a long day. In your case, this routine can be replaced by reading a book or by reading an online magazine or newspaper. You may even want to call your parents or siblings if you live away from home. It is not compulsory to have this included in your bedtime routine, but if you do decide to add this, it alludes to consistency and helps you sleep better. It helps you feel better and motivated for the next day.

You need to make it a habit to revisit your goals, at least once or twice a day to keep them fresh in your mind. Perhaps you have made some new year resolutions that you haven't followed through with yet. You need to revisit them each day for five minutes or less to remind yourself of them. You can do this by writing them down on a sticky note and pasting it on your refrigerator so that when you open it up in the morning, you'll be reminded of your resolution/goal. It helps to keep your habits in check. You will remain more disciplined and probably keep yourself away from any kind of useless activity. You will have an opportunity at the start of the day to check if you can get rid of any bad habits that are hindering you from achieving your goals. If you have set up a step-by-step plan to achieve your goals, you can double-check if you are following the steps and are not delineating from them (Kalish, n.d).

Experts believe that you should not make it a habit to skip breakfast because having a healthy breakfast helps you start the day off with more energy. Most people skip this meal because they say that they don't have sufficient time for it. As a result, this affects the entire schedule for the day. If you fail to gain sufficient energy and are slogging through the day, you will have a tough time and will be marked by a lack of productivity and positivity. Let me share a tip with you for a healthier breakfast. You can start the day off with a heavy food such as bread, butter, juices, honey, and milk. Lighten up the meals as the sun rises higher in the sky to complete its journey. A lighter meal for dinner will help you sleep better and wake up the next day with more energy. A higher level of energy at the start of each day means that you are happier than the day before. These upgrades in your habits seem to be small in size but their overall impact on your life are huge.

One other thing that is important is taking a break during your working hours. You need to make sure you rest during the day to be more productive and deliver your best efforts. Your workday will typically consist of small tasks and you have to keep switching from one task to another during the day. Don't get too involved in your work that you forget to take a break. Rest for a few minutes and then get back to work. Your brain needs a respite to function better. This habit will drive out accumulated stress from your brain and help you regain your concentration and focus. A break helps you do wonders in terms of boosting your productivity (Kalish, n.d).

# Boost Your Productivity

Productivity is something that is widely misunderstood by the masses. Productivity is used at both a micro and macro level. Sometimes, we refer to productivity as the aggregate output of workers from a factory. Here, I will talk about productivity at a personal level during which we have 100 percent control. We can boost our productivity when it seems to be slowing down and we can also tinker it to double what we can achieve in a single day. Personal productivity generally refers to the relevant output of a person during a specific period. Productivity defines the level of our growth and our living standards such as income and the quality of time.

The benefits of boosting productivity are as clear as water. When you work toward increasing your productivity, you are well on your way to getting better results in terms of product quality and monetary benefits. It means you are moving toward a higher level of growth. Productivity helps us innovate in our business. The 21st century is marked by a higher level of change because of the shifting demands of people and an industrial struggle to keep up with the demands. When you raise the levels of productivity, you get a major boost in the levels of innovation.

### Magical Rules to Boost Your Productivity

Have you ever wondered how some people are super productive during their day while others struggle with a single task? Elon Musk, Jeff Bezos, and Mark Zuckerburg are considered production machines. They are highly productive during all 24 hours of the day. Can you guess the reasons for such high levels of productivity? Are they blessed by God to be like that or is there something else that they have mastered to become this way? The secret is hidden in the study of their daily routine. Why do you think Mark Zuckerburg wears the same clothes every day? Why did Elon Musk sleep on the floor of his factory? If you know the answers to these simple questions, you know the secret to their productivity. Let's look at some helpful tips to make your day more productive.

1. Plan for each day: Race horses wear blinders so that they are not distracted during the race and their focus remains on crossing the finish line before other horses. We have to use the same techniques to save us from distractions that come our way during the race of life. We have to prioritize things to keep ourselves productive. Our focus ought to be ruthless and we must not heed to any kind of distractions. The reason why people like Elon Musk are successful is because they have clear priorities and they know what they need to focus on. It is not that their brains are naturally hardwired to follow their dreams but that they have prioritized their dreams over everything else. To them, work is more important than anything else. That's the secret to their success. You should learn to do things in the right order. If you have set a goal for yourself, you should put in the best effort to achieve that goal.

2.  Track your time: You need to track the time you are spending on each task during the day. Gauge how many minutes you have spent on a number of tasks such as preparing a report, editing a video, or producing content for social media campaigns. When you have calculated how much time you spend on each task, you can better plan out your day. You can better manage your time and see how quickly you are able to accomplish certain tasks.

3.  Take regular breaks: If you think working all day and night like a zombie can put you in the line of the most successful people in the world, you are wrong. If you work without respite, you are making yourself highly unproductive. This means that your work quality will be adversely affected. Learn to take short breaks during your work routine. When you take breaks, you cut down on stress levels, reduce fatigue, and do away with exhaustion. Now, you don't need to take hour long breaks. Your breaks can be as

short as five minutes to refuel your mind with fresh ideas and creativity.

4. Be your own boss: This one's important. Highly productive people don't wait for their boss to impose deadlines on them. They create their own world by setting deadlines for themselves and then rigorously follow them. Stress is a bad thing from the medical point of view but if it is at a manageable level, stress can push you to finish your work efficiently without harming you. Slight stress keeps you on track for accomplishing certain tasks within deadlines. Do not set deadlines for yourself if you know you cannot meet them. Learn to stick to deadlines that are achievable and you will be astonished to know how productive and focused you can become. Soon, your speed will increase and you will be able to meet deadlines at a much faster rate.

5. One task at a time: People who propound the theory of multitasking fool themselves

into thinking that they are machines, not humans. Our brain is not hard-wired for multi-tasking. In fact, various studies have alluded to how unproductive multitasking can be. The reason is simple. We cannot focus on a single thing when we are multitasking. It disrupts our focus and increases stress and fatigue. That is why we need to focus on one task at a time. To make the most out of this habit, you need to set your priorities straight. Establish what is most important and list your tasks in order of importance. Do not over-commit if your schedule doesn't allow it.

6. The two-minute rule: Experts believe that two-minutes is enough to give you a sense of the importance of time. You should set two-minute windows for small tasks and see how much progress you can make during that short window of time. There are lots of tasks that you can do in two minutes such as proofreading a draft, answering an email, and telephoning someone.

7. Plan each new day: You must plan your day the night before. Prepare to-do lists as they are a great productivity tool. Planning for each new day will allow you to stay well-organized in your work. Having a plan for the day allows you to start your day off right. Don't forget to keep your plan realistic or you will be left frustrated and annoyed with yourself.

## Optimize Your Environment

There are lots of studies that have been done to find out the best ways to optimize your work environment as well as the benefits of optimizing your work environment. If you want to be more productive, you ought to identify with the work environment and you also need to be able to adapt well with the different type of furniture that is being used in the office. You need to be able to boost your health and productivity at the office.

*Tweak Your Environment to Boost Productivity &*
*Better Learning*

The best way to make your work environment suitable to work in is to be able to work in a number of different places in the office. A single seating arrangement is unproductive because you will easily get bored during the day and will require a change of scenery. So, it is better to mix things up. Create multiple spots where you can work all day long.

If your work permits this, revamp your work environment every so often. You spend a good number of hours on the computer during your work schedule and this involves sitting at your desk for long hours. Take the time to explore other options to give your office a refreshing feel. Look into getting an adjustable desk; one where you can raise it and stand while you work to allow the blood flow properly to your legs. Although not very common, providing your team members with aerobic balls instead of chairs is another great option. Aerobic balls are in high demand because of the positive effect they have on the health of a user. They have a positive impact on the posture of an employee and likewise on their productivity.

If you are running a team of employees, you need to understand the nuances in their habits and abilities. Some people are morning people and they are more productive during the day while others are more productive during the afternoon. You need to figure out which employees work best during which hours. The next most important aspect for a workplace environment is the level of lighting. If the lighting is dull and shabby, the employees will feel sluggish and this will have a negative impact on their productivity levels. On the contrary, if the workplace is full of bright, natural lighting, it will keep the employees motivated and interested in their work. Coupled with the lighting scheme is the shape of the furniture that exists in your office. If you have arranged for rounded furniture, you will see an increase in productivity at the office. Angular furniture is marked with low levels of productivity. These kinds of matters may appear to be trivial in nature but in the long run, they have a huge impact on the overall productivity levels at your office.

Plants play an important role in your work environment as well. They are a brilliant way to create a welcoming and warm environment at your office both for the employees and your clients or business partners. They will feel at home upon each visit. The officials at the office will feel more alive which means they will be more productive as a result. If you add some artwork to your workspace, this will also boost productivity at the office. Include artwork that contains motivational words or phrases to keep the employees engaged while they work. A motivational piece of artwork works as a backdrop that operates on the subconscious levels of the employees and keeps them moving forward for greater innovation as well as efficiency.

If you want to optimize your workspace, you need to make sure that the overall energy levels of the office remain positive and optimistic and the employees always feel at home. Any kind of negative energy such as bad lighting, a dull piece of artwork, artifact, or plant that contains certain allergens must be removed from the office at the earliest opportunity. In addition to creating the ideal environment for your employees, your efforts will show the employees how much you care for their wellbeing. This will help to create a bond between you and your employees which is necessary for higher levels of productivity.

Another great way to optimize your work environment is to switch up the technology used in the office space. For example, you can buy your team the latest tech gadgets such as smart tablets and phones to work with in different corners of the office.

As a boss, you need to engage with your team in emotional terms. Leaders cannot be tyrannical. Show appreciation towards you colleagues if they have done something extraordinary for your company. Your staff will love you and appreciate you that much more if you show you care about the work they are contributing. You can arrange a dinner or a cup of coffee with the best-performing employee of the month as another way to show appreciation.

## Set Your Goals

How often do you feel the need to set goals? How often do you need to revisit what goals you have set earlier? Setting goals has its importance but what we don't realize is the fact that it is important to revisit them, rejuvenate them, and reinforce them along the way to the end destination. Goal setting is an exercise that is connected to the adoption of new behaviors. A goal is something that a person sets to attain in his or her life. In life, sometimes we are able to achieve goals and not achieve others and this contradiction is crucial to understand. We must learn to understand why achieving some goals is easier than others while our conviction levels remain almost the same. We can relate this problem to the existence of hurdles that stop us from achieving something in life. Goal setting helps us value the present moment and plan for the future. In this way, we can make good use of what we have in the present moment and also value the time we will have in the future. In a way, we are investing in our present and future to increase productivity. In addition to securing the time we have, goal-setting also motivates us along the way to the destination. When we cannot achieve a goal, it leads to frustration and low motivation levels. This means that we valued the time we had but sadly we wasted it in useless activities. This also gives us a lesson for the future to be careful and make good use of the time we have. If the conditions are right, goal setting can make you highly productive. It can turn out to be your secret weapon to success.

### How Setting Goals Improves Our Focus

Goal setting helps you achieve your goals because it increases your focus. Goals shape your behavior. In fact, they trigger good behavior. Getting into the habit of making clear and compelling goals helps you to mobilize your focus and also compels you to adopt actionable behavior that will be the source of your motivation. If you are working in a company that produces baby bottles, you may appear to be satisfied with life because your salary is taking care of your bills and your household expenditures. Can you explain what your goal is for joining the organization? Do you want a peaceful life by staying in a well-established company or do you want to gain experience for a few years and eventually move up the ladder to a higher position? You must be able to explain your goal right away upon asking. Only then you can say that you have set a goal for your life. If you cannot explain why you've set a certain goal, you essentially don't have a goal you are working towards. Without a goal in mind, you are just pushing through the days you have left in life. You can push through for a number of years but with each year gone, you will be left with a drier soul and broken spirit. You will gradually lose focus on the work you are doing because you don't have anything to strive for. This can really land you in trouble because companies are profit-driven and they only want those employees who are efficient workers.

If you have set a certain goal for your life, such as reaching the position of a Chief Executive Officer in a company, each step you take will lead you to that destination. You will find yourself being more attentive to new things that you must learn to achieve your goal. You will be willing to focus on any kind of training program that you attend. Your body will definitely follow your mind once you have agreed to set a goal for your life.

Who doesn't like progress? When you purchase a new car, your next goal is to buy a sports car. When you become an owner of an apartment, your next goal is to be an owner of a mansion or a luxury penthouse in Manhattan with a rooftop swimming pool and basketball court. Progress turns people into addicts. When you've achieved something in your life, you crave more. Your mind builds up momentum for making further progress to compel you to achieve more in life. When you see progress in one thing, you want to see progress in everything. You want to achieve more and more each time. One goal after another goal helps us maintain our focus on the final destination that must be achieved at all costs. If we don't have milestones to achieve, the whole task seems so gigantic that it instills fear in our hearts that is too powerful to beat single-handedly. Short milestones and goals help us achieve big tasks in a smooth and less nerve-wracking way. Goals define us as they build our personality and character. When you achieve a goal, you are proud of yourself for achieving something that may have been tough for you to achieve for various reasons. Achieving a goal means that you have defeated what made you once afraid. Goals build self-efficacy and confidence. No matter how humongous the task is, you need to convince yourself that by setting short goals, you can achieve it.

## How to Set up a Daily Routine for Higher Productivity Levels

There are a couple of things that can impact your productivity levels, your happiness, and also the trajectory of your career. These things are your habits. We've discussed in detail in earlier sections about what habits are. We've also discussed the importance of setting daily routines, sticking to them, and making that part of our habits. Our daily routines are important because they help us prioritize what is important for our careers and also help us eliminate any habits that have become a stumbling block in our way to building a successful career or life. A healthy daily routine helps make us more efficient. Now that we know routines have sizable importance in our lives, it is important to choose routines that will have a permanent place in our lives.

### *Prepare a List of Your Daily Tasks*

The first step toward creating a daily routine is to prepare a list of what you want to do in your life. You need to look into what you have to do each day. You must not worry about organizing the list in the first attempt. Just prepare the list and try to include all the daily tasks that you have on your mind and that you must accomplish. You can carry a notebook to jot down what you have to do in a day. Here's what you should include in your list:

- Write down the things you need to do before you go to work.
- Write down the things that you should do along the way to dropping your kids off at school.
- Write down the things that you need to do at the office.
- Write down the things that you have to do with respect to your exercise routine. This may include a walk, a running routine, a gym session, or a jogging session.
- Write down the things that must be done to ensure you eat healthy during the day. This includes buying groceries, cooking meals in the kitchen, preparing fresh juices, shopping for meat from the supermarket, etc.
- Include any errands you need to run on a particular day.
- Your daily routine may include tasks such as cleaning the house and taking out the trash.

- Include your reading routine; what you read in the morning and what you read before going to bed.

This is just an overview of what you need to include in your list. Your actual list may look longer than this and it may include repetitive tasks that you need to do on a daily basis. You may also add the following details to be more precise and efficient:

- Write down the details of your brushing time.
- Write down the details of how much time you want to give to your cooking in the kitchen.
- Write down the details of how much time you will give to reading.
- Write down the details of how much you have allocated to designing your product, marketing your product, and planning to launch it in the market.

You can delve into the details to make your list more precise and accurate. You can prepare a list for the entire week for the tasks that you are likely to repeat over and over again. Therefore, you can have two lists; one for the tasks that are likely to be repeated over the week and the other for the tasks that are to be included in each list such as meetings with clients and buying groceries, as these tasks aren't normally repeated on a daily basis. On the other hand, brushing your teeth and reading a book are examples of tasks that must be repeated each day.

### Set up a Schedule

You need to assess your energy levels and analyze which time of the day you feel most productive and energized. If you feel more energized in the afternoon, you should start scheduling in the afternoon. There is no need to start in the morning if you feel lazy in the morning. You will only waste your time and end up achieving nothing significant. Scheduling is important if you want to make the most out of your day. You need a morning routine if you are an early riser. Rising early and staying in bed like a sloth is not going to do you any good. Your attitude in the morning affects how the rest of your day will go. When the alarm rings, leave the bed instantly. This is what keeps most people from being productive. Rush to the bathroom, take a shower, brush your teeth, and prepare yourself a healthy breakfast. If you rise early, you will be able to accomplish a number of tasks that must be completed in the morning, such as dropping your kids off at school and reaching the office on time. Along the way, you may realize small tasks that you can add to your morning routine that will increase your productivity levels in the morning. This can include reading a book or cooking your kids' lunches so that you can have ample time to do other tasks when you get back home.

### The Evening Schedule

Your evening schedule matters a lot in shaping your mindset. The evening is for leisure time and you should stop any kind of revenue generating activity in the evening. Instead, cook dinner for your friends and family. Do something that keeps your mind away from the tasks at the office. If you let intrusive thoughts about some unfinished tasks at the office into your mind while you are not working, your levels of productivity will decrease. It will also add to your stress and depression levels. The human brain needs rest to keep stress levels in check, so don't think about your responsibilities at the office or anything unrelated to what you're experiencing in the present moment. When you have partied with friends and dined with family, you can quickly review how you are going to plan for the next working day before going to bed.

Some people complain that they don't have enough time during weekdays to do the things they love to do. If this is the case, take some time in the evening to take your pet dog out for a stroll or go out for a jog to ease away any stress you may be feeling. Make some time in your schedule to do something you enjoy. Here is a breakdown of some important things that you can do in the evening:

- You can have a chat on the phone with your friends.

- Meditate before going to sleep as it will relax your mind and body.

- Think about how tomorrow is going to be better than today and what you can do to ensure that happens.

- Read a book while in bed. It stimulates your brain and you will have a better sleep (Sanders, 2018).

## Manage Your Time Well

Time is a valuable resource that is usually lost because we cannot understand the importance of the seconds we have. It is not renewable, which means a second lost never comes back. We all have some past regrets for wasting precious time, but if we don't start valuing the time that is left, we will not be able to succeed in life. If we start managing our time efficiently, we will be able to accomplish the goals that we dream of. Everyone has a goal or a dream they wish to achieve. Only a handful of people are able to turn those dreams into reality because most people cannot give them the right amount of time to flourish. Millions of dreams, thousands of desires, and billions of goals go to waste because people can't find the time to materialize them. Just imagine what the world would look like if all the people on earth fulfilled their dreams and accomplished their goals. Most people, when they learn this reality, start respecting time but it is often too late to start. Time management is important both at a personal as well as professional level. You must learn basic time management skills to excel in life before you start losing this resource. Here is a breakdown of some top time management skills that you should consider if you want to accomplish your goals in time:

- You need to organize your time well if you want to succeed in life. Organization is the secret to success. This means that you should keep your living and work spaces neat and clean and in an orderly form so that you don't spend considerable time searching for things when you need them the most. In addition to saving time, an organized workspace and living space will help you ease off any stress levels.

- Experts believe that whatever comes in the written form is easy to implement. So, bring your goals and objectives into written form so that you may not have to recall them each time you want to revisit them. This includes your daily goals at the office or at home, or your weekly, monthly, or yearly goals. If you don't know where to start, you will waste considerable time on recalling how to kick off a task. You need to have written goals as well as objectives. In the absence of a written plan, people are in a fix for working on almost anything. They ask themselves a number of times whether they have to do something and how much time it is going to take.

- An important thing to consider is to manage your waiting time period. It happens to each of us when we have to wait for a train, a plane, or a bus. At some point, you will have to waste time that will not add value to your business or personal goals. You can use this time to catch up on things such as reviewing your progress in the past week and the amount of time your product is taking to make waves in the market. You can call a staff member to give them instructions on how to arrange a training session for your new employees. You can read a book in the meantime to add value to your character and knowledge base. You can think about a new version of your product. Yes, you can innovate during this time. Use your time efficiently. No matter what it is you're doing (Lotich, 2017).

## What Fears Stop You From Gaining Success?

There are different fears that hold us back from pursuing our dreams. These fears include the fear of being judged by people, the fear of failure, the fear of getting on the wrong track, and the fear of criticism. They are so common that almost everyone has experienced them. These fears kill many dreams across the globe. They compel people to procrastinate, distract them from their goals, and bury their heads in the sand so they cannot face reality. If you can deal with these fears and face them head on, you are well on your way to be a rocking star in life.

### Uncertainty

This is one of the biggest fears that holds us back when we conceive an idea. We are unaware of the dangers that lie ahead of us. We fear the unknown. You can kill this fear by anticipating the dangers you will face in the future. You can be proactive about dealing with them the moment they come your way. This is the only way to beat the fear of uncertainty.

### Fear of Failure

This fear is another hurdle you must overcome in order to succeed in life. This is why lots of people fail in life despite having the ability to succeed. You have to convince yourself that the most beautiful places on earth are only accessible through the most dangerous and difficult roads. You must learn to weather the storm when you face one. You can plan for future ventures to minimize the chances of failure. A carefully built plan can help you tackle failures head on. Make a prediction of future failures so that you may not be caught by surprise when they happen.

### Fear of Rejection

The third most lethal fear that kills lots of dreams before they mature is the fear of rejection. We always fear that people will not approve of what we are doing. For example, you are an employee at a top company and you receive a handsome salary each month to feed yourself and your family. You can plan a vacation out of the money you receive from the company you work in. Something most people dream of. However, you have a dream of starting your own production business. Your biggest fear is that you're afraid of being rejected by society. You fear what people will say about you leaving a well-paying job. How will they react when they find out? This kills the passion in your heart. If you want to keep moving in pursuance of your dreams, you must beat this fear. The most feasible way to do that is to pay less heed to the people around you. Let them talk and they will keep quiet after a while. Follow your dreams despite what others think or say.

# Chapter 3: An Overview of Fears

I have given you a peek into what fears are and what forms they appear in. Fears are of different kinds. Out of all of them, the biggest is the fear of the unknown. We come out of our shell for a while to announce that we will fight the circumstances to change our life, when suddenly, a fear grips us so hard that we put an end to our plans, and we rush back to where we came from. Most people have brilliant ideas in their minds to challenge the status quo, but they lack the courage to break the chains that have bound them. I am not saying that these fears are illegitimate and all the people who fall prey to them are cowardly, but what I want to explain is that these fears are responsible for failures in the world. These fears keep people from stepping up to do what they always wanted to do. This chapter carries details on emotions and fears and also the ways to deal with them.

# What Are Emotions?

This question is simple and I am sure you know the answer to it as well. What if you are asked to define what emotions are. Will you be able to define them? Each person has a different definition of what emotions are. Every person perceives a single situation in a different way. Some find a kid playing piano attractive, other sonorous and a few people find it provoking. Emotions are basically intense feelings that can be linked to situations, both real and imaginary.

Emotions are packages of messages that your brain prepares and sends to the entire body, signaling to you if there is a threat or a happy experience. These messages direct your body to provide a physical reaction like a round of applause or laughter. If you perceive a threat, it interprets it, and sends a message to your body to give a suitable reaction like running away from the site of threat or preparing yourself to face the threat.

***Types of Basic Emotions***

In this section, I will explain what the basic types of emotions are. There are different types of emotions that can affect how you live and interact with the world around you. Our emotions rule over our bodies and our actions. They exert a hefty influence on the types of choices we make, the types of actions we choose, and our perceptions as well. All these things are greatly influenced by the kind of emotions we harbor at any moment. Psychologists have worked day and night to find out the basic types of emotions that are most common in people. The list is a short one, but a meaningful one, because these emotions rule over our bodies while we conduct our daily lives.

1. Gloom or Sadness: It is something that is prevalent in our society. This emotion is characterized by feelings of grief, disappointment, disinterest, and hopelessness. Sadness is almost experienced by everyone regardless of age and gender, though its intensity differs for

different age groups. You can express this emotion in a variety of ways such as lethargy, quietness, loneliness, and crying. The intensity of sadness depends on the severity of the incident that caused that emotion. For example, if you have lost your cell phone on a subway, you will remember the incident for a short time and feel sad about it. It is hardly likely that you will cry about it. Even if you do cry, the memory will be for a short timespan. On the other hand, if you lose a loved one, the emotion of sadness will prevail over you for a longer time. You will feel lonely, sad, and weak for the days to come.

2. Fear: Fear is another powerful emotion that overpowers people at times. It is so powerful that it can play a big role in your survival. When you face some kind of danger and feel fear, you are faced with two choices: you either run away or stay and fight the danger. This is called the fight or flight response. Fear causes tense muscles,

a faster heart rate, and a rapid rise in respiration, and it makes your mind stay alert to any kind of noise or movement. The response triggered by this emotion defines who you are and how you are going to deal with some uncanny and unexpected situation. Fear can cause you to wear special expressions on your face such as widened eyes and a pale complexion. Either you will seek cover to hide or you will flee the scene. Other reactions include faster breathing and a higher pulse rate. Some people despise being in fearful situations while others love it because of the adrenaline they feel.

3. Happiness: This is an emotion that everyone in the world has experienced at least once before. It is the emotion that is most accepted and appreciated by most people. It brings about feelings of contentment, satisfaction, health, joy, and gratitude. Research on the emotion of happiness has significantly increased over

the last few years. You can tell a person is happy if he or she is smiling, their body language is relaxed, and their tone is pleasant. Happiness can come from listening to music, offering prayers, reading your favorite book, hearing the news of the promotion of your son or daughter, hearing the news of the birth of your grandchild, winning a lottery ticket, or buying a new home for your family.

### Techniques to Master Your Emotions

You can master your emotions if you keep your body in a perfect balance. You can do this by eating healthy food, regularly exercising, and getting enough sleep daily. You might be thinking that all these things are compulsory for a normal life. Yes, that's right. Why I have mentioned them here is because of the fact that a healthy body can guarantee a positive and healthy emotional life. Experts believe that moving your body can help improve your predictions about your future. Besides eating a healthy diet, you should spend some time in nature, practice yoga or meditation, and also have full-body massages. Reading also perfectly balances out your emotions. If we look at emotions through a spiritual lens, we may say that social contact and the habit of giving also add balance to your emotions.

You should develop the habit of being a collector of multiple experiences. Each new experience that comes from watching movies, reading new books, trying out new types of food, or adding new words to your vocabulary, carry opportunities for you to build upon your life. When your brain has a stream of new concepts, you will be able to build robust emotional health. A fresh stream of knowledge and the latest concepts will aid in dealing with different circumstances. It also improves your negotiation skills.

As I have already mentioned in the past chapters, our brain is hardwired to remember only negative emotions. Negativity takes its toll on our emotional health. The memories, feelings, and the concepts that catch our attention, are automatically reinforced in our brains. We remember them more often and they keep affecting our emotional health. If we rewire our brain to remember only positive thoughts and emotions, we will be able to leave a positive impact on our emotional health. This practice cultivates the way for any future positivity that comes your way. The easiest way to remember positive emotions is by writing them on a piece of paper and then recalling them later on to refresh your memory.

## What Is Fear?

Fear is one of the most common emotions that people experience. It is caused by something that threatens your life, your loved ones, your friends, your wealth, your health, or your brain. I have already explained this emotion in the past sections of this book. You can kill fear by getting rid of the source of fear. For example, you can work hard to attain financial security to eliminate the fear of poverty. All things considered, the fact is that fear has the power to paralyze your brain and overpower your ability to think and make decisions.

### What Causes Fear?

Fear has different triggers. They could be triggers from school, work, family life, you name it. For example, if you hit someone at school and you expect them to retaliate, the emotion that is going to govern you is labeled as fear. The threat can also be psychological such as the fear of ghosts or spirits. Another common fear is the fear of the dark. People who suffer from clinical depression despise social interactions as they fear that people will reject them. Some people fear different animals and reptiles. The sight of a rodent, snake, or any other wild animal sends chills up their spine. The fear of death is another common one, as we are not in control of how and when we are going to die or how and when others will die.

When we don't know the source of our fear, we become afraid because we don't know how to remove it from our vicinity.

*How Does Fear Work?*

Our brain is a complex organ that consists of over 100 billion nerve cells that form a complex network. There are innumerable areas in the brain that play a key role in transferring information. Dozens of areas in the brain are involved in creating fear in your brain. Research shows that there are different parts of the brain that play key roles in this entire process. These parts include the following:

Thalamus: This part of the brain decides how the incoming information from different sensors such as the skin, eyes, ears, and mouth ought to be handled and redirected to the necessary sections of the brain.

Sensory cortex: This part of the brain does the job of interpreting the data the Thalamus receives from body sensors.

Hippocampus: This part of the brain plays the role of storing and retrieving conscious memories in addition to processing stimuli for establishing context.

Amygdala: This part of the brain bears the responsibility of decoding your emotions and determines if a threat exists or not. It also stores the memories that are linked to fear.

Hypothalamus: This part of the brain has the power to activate the response system. It directs you to either run away from the source of fear or stand like a rock and combat the source to neutralize the threat (Layton, n.d).

### *Fear Can Be Your Greatest Asset*

Up until now, we've talked about the negative impacts that fear can have on your mind and your body; but the fact remains that most fears are good for you. Fear works as a security system in our brain to make us aware of the dangers that exist around us. It keeps us out of life-threatening situations. Yes, we must remain afraid of certain dangers in the world. Take the example of a busy intersection that has a lot of traffic all hours of the day. If you are not fearful of being hit by a big truck, you would casually cross the road and likely get hit by a truck because you crossed when you shouldn't have. However, because most of us do fear that we will be hit if we cross at the wrong time, then that is why we do not cross and follow the rules. It is the fear of becoming poor and homeless that drives us out of the comforts of our beds in the morning and keeps us engaged in work. We cannot stop working despite knowing the fact that we are extremely tired, and the work is robbing us of the joys of life. If we are not afraid of harming the public image of our brand, we will not care about the quality of the product that reaches the hands of consumers.

It is common for people to be fearful when they are about to deliver a public presentation. One option to get over this kind of fear is to rename or redirect it. You can convince yourself that it is just an adrenaline rush or a moment of excitement. Name your fear. Name it something that excites you. Use it to stay motivated for the public presentation you have to put on. You need to channel your feelings of fear into making your speech more expressive, fiery, and engaging.

We are all fearful of what can happen in the future. This fear is at its highest when we are on the verge of starting a new business or a new product. Or, perhaps, even when getting married, starting a new relationship, etc. We are afraid that people will reject our ideas or we fear that we fail in trying to run the business out of lack of funds. What if we are unable to pay our bills? What happens if we don't find a way out when we get stuck in an entrepreneurial venture? What happens when we quit our full-time job to start a new business? Fear is what keeps people working eighteen hours a day. It is this fear that keeps them on the edge and makes them succeed in the end. It is this fear that takes them to the top of the world. Still, too much fear of something is not good for your mental and physical health. You must overcome it if you want to find success in your life.

***How to Overcome Your Fears?***

The best technique to overcome your fears is to face them head-on. If you keep avoiding situations that instill fear in your heart, you won't be able to succeed in your life. Face what scares you. If you are afraid of how you will manage your finances if you leave your full-time job and start your freelance career, you should tackle this problem head-on by calculating your steps and then jumping right in. If you are unwilling to leave the bay, you will never be able to taste what adventure the waves of the sea have for you. Keep in mind that only those people who succeed in life have done so because they stepped up and left their comfort zones.

# Chapter 4: Live a Happier Life

Happiness is more of a mindset than something that you can buy or get from anyone else. It is an attitude that comes after you banish pessimism from your brain and welcome optimism with all its blessings. It may seem that the answer to this complex question is trapped in your attitude toward life, but in reality, it is more or less concerned with the chemical processes that exist in your brain. If you happen to be leaning toward pessimism and are caught in the web of hopelessness, you will be glad to know that optimism is an attitude you can achieve after diligent training. In this chapter, I'll explain the importance of optimism and how it can help you in your life. I will also talk about the importance of taking care of your health. You will learn how you can be a better version of yourself and how you can cultivate joy. In addition, you will also learn how meditation can help you streamline your life.

# How to Train Your Brain to Be an Optimist

When you are struggling with life, it seems impossible to be optimistic about anything. Pessimism seems inevitable at times. You feel caught in the grip of negativity and pessimism with such a force that you become hopeless about getting yourself extricated from the claws of hopelessness. Optimistic people are happier, creative, and innovative. They are more likely to solve complex problems than average people. They have gained an elevated level of mental alertness in comparison to people who have harbored pessimism for a lot longer. Optimists also are less stressed than pessimists because they have lower levels of cortisol, which is the hormone that releases stress. Here is a break down of the ways by which you can keep yourself optimistic all the time ("8 ways to Train Your Brain to Be More Optimistic," n.d).

- Practice self-care on a daily basis. This means that you must find ways to relax your nervous system. Find means to control and relax your breathing and heart rate. Other ways you can relax your nervous system include yoga and meditation. By practicing yoga, deep breathing, meditation, or taking a bath, you are on your way to finding happiness in doing small tasks. Your stress levels will decrease and you will be more optimistic about life ("8 ways to Train Your Brain to Be More Optimistic," n.d).

- Laughter is considered to be the best medicine. It is fantastic in what it is capable of doing. Belly laughs have the power to induce the production of serotonin that calms the amygdala, the stress center of your brain. You can play your favorite comedies on television or you can try laughter yoga ("8 ways to Train Your Brain to Be More Optimistic," n.d).

# Don't Let Negativity Destroy Your Confidence

Who doesn't experience negative thoughts? Almost everyone on the earth experiences them. The only difference is that some people don't let negative thoughts stop them from doing what they need to do, while others have not properly trained their minds to simply let them go. Some psychologists say that the story of human life is, in fact, a tale of the battle with negativity. How well we fight these thoughts and how well we conquer them define us and shape us as humans.

Normally, when you feel sad, you really can't explain the root of the problem. You say that you are sad but you are unable to explain what has caused this negative feeling in you. The very first step to killing negative thoughts is to trace their roots. Negative thoughts originate from self-doubt. Whenever we try to accomplish something big, all incidents of when we have failed before come back to haunt us. What we fail to understand is the fact that our self-doubt is the result of our intelligence.

Before tackling any challenge, our brain decides to analyze the situation and consider all possible dangers that may come our way. Early humans could only evolve in lethal environments because they had a tendency to perceive dangers before they even happened. They were continuously threatened by wild ferocious animals, rival humans, and natural disasters. That's why a continuous watch on the expected dangers hardwired their brains to look out for dangers in all situations. This means that these negative thoughts are just a sign that our brain is analyzing the situation and sensing all the possible dangers that may not even materialize at all. So, there is no point in chasing them madly.

The second step is to keep yourself away from the source of negativity in your life. You need to boost your confidence to fight off negative thoughts effectively. Prepare a list of the strengths you have and the tasks you have accomplished so far and that you are proud of. You should add to this list regularly. Keep challenging yourself with a fresh new activity like doing yoga, practicing meditation, cooking for your wife and parents, reading a new book, writing a new song, or cycle through your favorite streets in the city. Do whatever makes you feel positive about yourself. If you are not regularly exercising, start doing that right away. Take care of your sleep. Keep telling yourself self-affirmative statements on a daily basis. Tell your conscious self that you are a fighter, a good writer, a confident person, a vocalist, a fitness enthusiast. You can include in the list all the qualities that you have. Don't ignore them; appreciate them. Appreciate yourself.

## How to Open Your Mind With Books

Are you fond of reading books, magazines, or newspapers? Or are you, like many other people, in the habit of reading tweets, Facebook posts, and Instagram posts? If you don't value books, you are missing out on some of the greatest benefits that reading books may offer you. Different studies show that if your brain remains stimulated, it can slow down the progress of Dementia or

Alzheimer's disease because your brain remains active and engaged. Your brain, just like any other muscle in the body, requires proper exercise to stay strong. Your brain views books as puzzles that it has to solve, and puzzles and games like chess, that challenge the brain, keep the brain healthy.

### Benefits of Reading Books

Reading books is beneficial for a number of reasons. Reading a book can you help you forget about the enormous levels of stress you may have experienced during your work day or in your familial or personal relationships. Immerse yourself into a great story to forget about all your troubles. Grab a novel written by Charles Dickens and you will forget what is happening around you. He is a Victorian Classic novelist and you might consider his books outdated. Let it be. He will take you for a ride into the Victorian world. What is best about Charles Dickens is his sense of humor. Even a business best-seller has the power to divert your mind from your current environment and redirect you to the world of fantasy. A good book will drain out stress and allow relaxation and happiness into your mind.

Books help you gain immense knowledge about different things. If you are reading a novel, you will learn about human behavior. A business book will give you insight into the business world while an autobiography of a business tycoon will give you inspiration for achieving something significant in your life. More knowledge means you have more power to take on the world, and it will also help you get through challenging moments (Winter, 2019).

## Never Stop Working on Yourself

The key to changing your mindset is to do things that were once a challenge for you. For example, if you have not participated in a singing competition but you know that you can sing, put on your big girl pants and hit the stage. Even if you are rejected, you have the satisfaction that you have participated in the competition, and you have taken that first step toward turning your goal into a reality.

## *Be a Better Version of Yourself*

You can make yourself a better person by creating an original vision for yourself. Your unique vision is what makes you better than others and your previous self. Another trick is to realize the fact that there is no secret to making yourself a better you. You have to give yourself the time that is required by your mind and body to improve on what you already have and who you already are.

You can be a better version of yourself by improving your social network. Interact with influential people through Facebook and Twitter and make your dream a reality. Read what they have to say about life and the business world and gain inspiration. Then, create your own ideas and float them before people to read and get inspired.

Sometimes, we want to achieve something big in our lives and in the quest to get that, we ignore small opportunities that cross our path. It is not impossible to gain knowledge of any skills that are a hot commodity in the market. Knowledge is no longer locked away in the brains of top experts in certain industries. Anyone can learn a skill through an online course or by purchasing the best book on a particular topic. When you work on improving yourself, you are becoming a better version of your present self.

You should learn to celebrate small wins and appreciate what you are doing in the present moment. It will keep you motivated and you will achieve more. It will help you set higher goals.

## Cultivating Joy

Happiness comes from a number of external sources and they are all temporary. On the other hand, joy is different. Joy is something divine, and it shapes the way you express yourself before others. When you have found a purpose in life, you are joyful because you have found a reason for your existence. You are on your way to fulfilling a mission in your life. Joy can come from reading a book, meeting a childhood friend, or by surrounding yourself with family. Whatever rejuvenates your spirit, keep doing that to cultivate joy in your life.

### Ways to Cultivate More Joy in Your Life

The best way to cultivate joy in your life is to help others. It always feels great to help someone who is in need or support a cause that is meaningful to you. When you are helping someone out, you are doing that from the core of your heart. An act of altruism is a reminder that you have done something that is more important and bigger than yourself. It tells you that there are bigger things happening in the world. Not only that, but it also helps to cut down on stress and anxiety levels. A win-win situation if you ask me.

There are always going to be people who will complain about what they don't have or why they have less of something than someone else. Every human being has a typical thought process that he or she lets flow through the brain each day. This thought process remains the same each day and is often the source of negativity and sadness. Most of these thoughts are negative, that's why you need to change them. The best way to change your thought process is to practice gratitude. Think about all that you have in your life. This could be anywhere from the roof over your head to your loving spouse to the high-paying job you just got offered. We don't quite understand that but the fact remains that our thoughts shape our actions, and if the thoughts don't change, our actions remain the same. When we change our thoughts, we are able to form a new pattern for our actions. Practicing gratitude can help us shift our perspective and improve our mood.

## Take Care of Your Health

Poor health is connected to an increased level of stress because our brain is always in a quest to fight off whatever diseases or illnesses we may be harboring. Poor health makes even simple daily tasks a challenge as it escalates our health expenses and jeopardizes our ability to earn a handsome living. Maintaining a healthy lifestyle means we will have decreased levels of stress and that will have a positive effect on whatever we do in life.

The first step towards living a healthy lifestyle is to eat a healthy diet. Also, make a commitment to yourself that you will eat the foods that will boost your energy levels and will also keep your systems functional in all circumstances. When you feel healthier, you will be able to take on bigger challenges which are really helpful for managing your stress levels. People who suffer from malnutrition are more reactive to stressful situations, so make sure whatever you include in your diet will help relieve stress. Some of the most common and overlooked rules for a healthy diet include eliminating junk food and consuming fresh fruits and green leafy vegetables. What you eat directly affects your mood, so if your diet is poor, it will have a bad effect on your mood. If you are eating a healthy diet, you will surely be in a much lighter and happier mood. You will no doubt feel more optimistic and energized. Eating right is the best thing that you can do for yourself, your mind, and your body. All of this will have a direct effect on your life.

Staying healthy doesn't mean that you should only consume the right food; it also means that you should get enough sleep during the night. Less sleep means that you are less productive and less mentally sharp. We should be getting between seven to eight hours of sleep every night. If you recognize that you get less than seven or eight hours of sleep at night, make sure you make the change immediately. Getting enough sleep will put you on a healthier life track, and it will also restore your confidence and happiness levels.

The best way to stay healthy is to follow a routine that works best for you. This routine may include vigorous exercise such as lifting weights, or light exercise such as going for a light jog. Health, once lost, takes its toll on our intimate as well as professional life; therefore, it is best to reform your eating and workout routine immediately to lead a happier and healthier life.

# Science-Based Benefits of Meditation

Meditation involves the habitual training of your mind so that you can focus on what you are doing and redirect your thoughts to be more constructive about your life and your experiences. People meditate to develop beneficial habits and to cultivate softer feelings that will transform their mood from good to bad. People also meditate in order to acquire self-discipline. Meditation also helps you in streamlining your sleeping patterns and increases your tolerance for pain. Here is a rundown of some scientific benefits of meditation:

- Meditation helps to reduce stress. Physical and mental stresses are due to an increase in the production of cortisol, a stress hormone, in your brain. Stress furthermore is harmful to your brain because it tends to release cytokine which is an inflammation-provoking chemical. Meditation will reduce the stress in your brain and body which in turn will help improve your sleeping patterns and blood pressure.

- Meditation improves your emotional health, which is necessary for you to be able to cultivate a positive image of your life. Cytokines, an inflammatory chemical, is released due to stress. If you don't control it, it will land you in depression. As mentioned earlier, meditation regulates the flow of cytokines, and in this way it reduces depression.

- Meditation helps you achieve a state of control and focus. When we are practicing meditation, we focus on only one thing at a time. This could be on our breath or a single thought. That is the act of meditation. Mindful awareness is an integral part of meditation, hence, the same quality of mind helps us deal with our daily life problems as well. This increased amount of focus can be used in studies, work, and relationships. Meditation can help you through anything.

# Chapter 5: Aim for the Next Level

Most people in this world work a job that pays enough to be able to feed themselves and their families. They are happy with their current job because it doesn't challenge them to leave their comfort zone and expose themselves to certain challenges or hazards of life. However, is this the right approach to take? Are you able to grow in life if you remain in your comfort zone? The answer is simply, no. The relish of a life is in the adventure. In this chapter, I will explain the traits of a leader with a growth mindset and the ways to improve a business mindset. I will also explain the mindset of a champion and the techniques to achieve this mindset. The chapter ends on a note about the power of a growth mindset in order to change the course of your love life.

# Business: Mindset and Leadership

Employees of different organizations are constantly being told that they must check the to-do list of what is to be accomplished each day. If people get stuck doing the same tasks over and over again each day, it becomes repetitive and also very boring. Employees will grow tired of their work as a result. As a result, they also have little room to evolve as a leader and an entrepreneur. A desire keeps burning in their hearts like a flame that they should lead others in the business world. The reason why most of us cannot be leaders is that we are unable to break free from certain chains that bind our brains. We are resistant to change and stepping out of our comfort zones.

### Traits of a Leader With a Growth Mindset

1. A growth mindset demands that leaders ought to be inclusive of the needs of others. They must keep an open mind that welcomes criticism and suggestions from others. A growth mindset demands that

leaders focus on sales and generation of revenue. They should have a clear understanding of what the needs of the human capital are and how to fulfill them to make them more productive. Leaders with a growth mindset need to serve the unique needs of individual clients and consumers along with the employees.

2. Entrepreneurs always have to deal with uncertain situations in terms of profits and losses and many other things such as the loss of a precious human resource. As a leader, you need to allow risk to have a permanent place in your heart and your business. If you want to compete with others and also want to be the best, you must learn to deal with ambiguity and see through it to discover endless opportunities for not only your business but your life in general. Each time leaders face an uncertain situation, they step back for a moment to discover the nature of uncertainty and determine how they can turn it into

something positive. Also, leaders should teach their staff to kill their fear of uncertain situations as well. It's just a part of life.

3. Leaders never jump into a situation without preparing for it first. They analyze the pros and cons of each situation beforehand. They consume a lot of time and money on planning before entering the operational phase. That's why top entrepreneurs succeed in launching a product and making it successful. People fail because they are not very well prepared for any untoward incident in their business venture. Leaders defy this behavior and this is what makes them different from others.

4. Leaders have a clear mind. They can see things more clearly than others. If a problem occurs in the marketing campaign of a product, leaders are more likely to ferret out the root of the problem as compared to other employees. Not only do they have the tendency to find out the problem faster but they also have the solution to fix the

problem and normalize the situation. In some cases, they act proactively and prevent a problem from happening in the first place. They pay close attention to the decisions they make and the shortcomings of those decisions, and they likewise come up with the most viable solutions to remove the shortcomings and make the decisions impeccable.

5. Leaders don't stay alienated from their employees. In fact, they love to grow with people by working directly with them, communicating with them, and getting feedback from them in regard to certain decisions that have been made.

### Ways to Improve Your Business Mindset

There are lots of people who prefer managing their own business over working full-time jobs, despite the fact that they have the right capabilities and skills for some top-level jobs. When they are starting their own business, they forget to take into consideration some key details such as how the consumers will view their business and how the products will impact the population as a whole. In order to build a successful business from scratch, you must be able to cultivate a business mindset. If you are running a photo editing company, you need to understand the modern demands of this business such as the right tools and the latest services that are hitting the markets each day. If you cannot keep up with the latest changes in the market, you cannot grow because your competitors will surpass you in everything you do. That's why you need to focus on the why factor. Why are you running this business? Is it your passion or a time-pass? Are you doing this out of some compulsion or are you eyeing the top slot in the world of entrepreneurship? Do you want to keep making both ends meet or do you want to be a billionaire? When fears engulf your brain and you are about to swerve from your path, the answers to these questions will help you remain on the right track.

Leaders are always in learning mode. This might seem ridiculous but this is essential for leaders to grow. Elon Musk, CEO of SpaceX and Tesla, is always bent on learning new things. Ashlee Vance writes in the autobiography of Elon Musk that Musk was a great learner and listener. He knew the basics of rocket science but didn't know the advanced technology. He hired top engineers and made them speak on different topics while he listened to them. Ashlee says that Musk seemed to have absorbed the knowledge of those engineers. Warren Buffett is also known to read around 500 pages per day. This includes newspapers, magazines, business reports, and stock market reports. Bill Gates is known to be a voracious reader of books. President Barack Obama is a voracious reader of books as well. Notice a pattern here? Leaders are always in learning mode. They are never shy of it, and this is what makes them great at running businesses and leading nations (Vance, 2015).

If you want to be a great business leader, you must establish a daily routine for all your tasks. You should have a set time to wake up, to work-out, to practice yoga, to meditate, to eat, and to work. If you don't have a routine, you are unlikely to make it to the other end of the tunnel. A solid routine allows one to be more productive in whatever you are doing. It helps you manage your time well and accomplish your daily goals.

## Sports: The Mindset of a Champion

Are you a soccer fan? If you are, you must admire some of the greatest players of all time like Christiano Ronaldo, Messi, and Neymar. All three are well-known and immensely successful as footballers. There are millions of people across the world who want to be like them, but they cannot be like them because they don't have the required stamina and the mindset to beat the odds that cross their path. You have to start with yourself. You have to make yourself a top priority. You have to bring some concrete changes in your life that will help you climb the ladder of success. If you are adamant on change, you will not be able to achieve what you dream of.

*How to Develop a Champion Mindset*

The very first trait of people who have a champion mindset is that they are highly committed to what they are doing. Practicing for more than 15 hours a day is not that easy. If you are prone to distractions, you cannot reach your destination. Commitment is important when it comes to achieving a target in your life. It keeps the view of the destination lucid so that you cannot take your eyes off of it. Commitment should not only be about hitting the target but it should also be about maintaining the quality of work you are doing. You must also be able to keep in view the time period in which you have to finish the task. You need to be able to identify what your end goal is, how you are going to get there, and how much time you need to get there.

Champions are always highly disciplined when it comes to achieving a goal. They streamline their targets and the strategies to deal with hurdles. They strategize whenever they see a decline in their performance. If you want to change your mindset and attain a champion mindset, you should surround yourself with positive people who will help you see things with a clear lens. Surround yourself with people who motivate you in life, not bring you down. Eliminate those who are not pushing you towards your goal and instead are dragging you down or are inflicting doubting thoughts in your mind about what you can and can't do. Dig out any bad seeds before they turn into cancer. Eliminate any limiting beliefs you have about yourself and your ability to achieve your goals. Replace your negative thoughts with positive ones and notice the difference you feel after doing this. Bring positive people into your circle of friends. Those who will help you grow and motivate you. Those who will help you adopt new habits that will aid you in achieving your targets and goals.

Have you ever started work with full zeal and zest but then the spirit that prevailed at the start of the task faded away slowly? Has this ever happened to you? I can assure you it has happened to everyone at least once, if not more times. Commitment and discipline can do nothing for you if you lack consistency in your work. Consistency can be defined as doing something over and over again in the same manner and consistency. It requires that the quality of whatever you're doing remains the same. If your quality is fluctuating, you are inconsistent, and this drives away customers from your business outlets. You will have to suffer from big losses if you remain inconsistent.

Champions understand the importance of life. They know that failure becomes inevitable in most occasions of life. What makes them stand out among the rest of the lot is their reaction to failure. They craft a plan and make it work to compensate for the losses that were incurred due to the failure. One quality that distinguishes them from others is that they don't play the blame game when they fail. They take responsibility for what happened and then make efforts to change the results.

They have a unique power to get over their losses quickly. They reflect on the number of losses and try to learn from them. They don't set out to mourn for what they have lost. Instead, they are optimistic about future outcomes and that's what makes them different from others.

## Power of Growth Mindset to Shift the Course of Love

Everyone wants a romantic relationship, but they don't want to put in the effort that is needed to build a healthy relationship. An understanding of your mindset will affect how you take care of your relationships. With a fixed mindset, you will feel an unstoppable urge to prove yourself in front of others and make yourself seem successful. You will feel that some people are just born equipped with the skills to manage relationships. So, when you have to put in effort to streamline your relationships, you will feel as if you are incompetent. You will convince yourself that you don't have the natural power to create meaningful relationships with others and, therefore, view yourself as incapable of forming them in the first place.

Every relationship has to go through bumpy roads and if your relationship hits a speed breaker, you will lose interest in walking ahead and start the blame game. On the contrary, a person who has a growth mindset will take up all the challenges that accompany a relationship and he or she will see bumps as opportunities to increase their learning. He or she will use their capacity to love throughout their lifetime. People with growth mindsets will always be on the lookout for opportunities that could deepen their relationships with others, be it family or a spouse. Those with a growth mindset will enjoy the course their relationship takes. They will be curious about what the next day brings for their relationship with others and they will not fester on the thought of what if things go wrong.

# Conclusion

If you want to have more fun in life and you want to enjoy it to the fullest, you must change your mindset from a fixed mindset to a growth mindset. It has the power to impact your success, career, and health. Your mindset is an opinion that you have about yourself. It is what you think of your abilities and competencies. There are lots of studies that show that people are not good at making an estimate of their abilities, but history has witnessed that those who are able to achieve tremendous successes in life are the ones who have the talent for identifying their strengths and weaknesses. As I have discussed in the last chapter, people who have a fixed mindset are not great at keeping up healthy relationships. They want to be with someone who will unconditionally worship them and ignore whatever bad they do. Or, they will ignore the red flags that rise in the other person because they don't want to avoid any challenges they may face in their relationship. They think that the other person should be able to read their minds. They also believe that there is no such thing as a disagreement between lovers or friends, and if something like that happens, they must immediately run away from the relationship.

In this book, you have learned how beneficial it is to have a growth mindset over a fixed mindset and how you can achieve all the good in your life just by changing your mindset. I have also explained to you how a fixed mindset can bar you from exploring your full potential and how it can keep you from exploring your talents.

There is no shortage of people on the earth who fail to achieve anything significant in life just because they couldn't change their minds. They die as the same person they were born because they didn't muster up the courage to defeat their own mindsets. They remain pessimistic and fail all the time. They fail in relationships and in their businesses. They are financially weak because they don't have the courage to build up a business even when they have the resources laid out in front of them. They don't see the positives in everything they do and everything they have, and instead focus only on the negatives.

I wrote this book in hopes of putting an end to a negative mindset. I wrote it to eliminate the existence of a fixed mindset. I hope to bring about a change in society with the help of this book.

I have comprehensively explained the symptoms that indicate a fixed mindset. If you think you have a fixed mindset, make sure you look over the points in this book that determine what encompasses a fixed mindset and what encompasses a growth mindset. This book has provided you with a variety of methods and techniques that you can follow and adopt to bring about a change in your life. I hope that after reading this book you are able to identify the difference between what a positive mindset can do for you and what a negative one will do. Keep in mind that everyone has the same type of mind. It's just a matter of how you choose to use your mind. It is our circumstances that shape what we become and how we view the world. More than the circumstances, it is how our mind reacts to different situations that shape our mindset. I want you to train your mind to see the positive in every situation. Best of luck!

# References

8 ways to Train Your Brain to Be More Optimistic, (n.d). Retrieved from https://www.livestrong.com/article/1012092-5-ways-train-brain-optimistic/

Becker, J. (n.d). 10 Tips to Start Living in the Present Moment. Retrieved from https://www.becomingminimalist.com/10-tips-to-start-living-in-the-present/

Kalish, A. (n.d). 16 Small Ways You Can Improve Your Life in Less than 30 Minutes. Retrieved from https://www.themuse.com/advice/16-small-ways-you-can-improve-your-life-in-less-than-30-minutes

Khan, A. (2017). 5 Influential Ways to Turn Failure Into Success. Retrieved from https://addicted2success.com/success-advice/5-influential-ways-to-turn-failure-into-success/

Layton, J.. (n.d). How Fear Works. Retrieved from

https://science.howstuffworks.com/life/inside-the-mind/emotions/fear.htm

Lotich, P. (2017). 12 Time Management Tips – Do You Manage Your Time Well? Retrieved from https://thethrivingsmallbusiness.com/12-time-management-tips-do-you-manage-your-time-well/

Maxwell, J. (2014). 5 Surefire Ways to Sharpen Your Skills. Retrieved from https://www.johnmaxwell.com/blog/5-surefire-ways-to-sharpen-your-skills/

Patel, D. (2019). 10 Powerful Ways to Master Self-Discipline. Retrieved from https://www.entrepreneur.com/article/287005

Sanders, S. (2018). How to Establish a Daily Routine to Become Your Best Self. Retrieved from https://www.goalcast.com/2018/11/26/establish-daily-routine-become-best-self/

The Importance of Failure: 5 Valuable Lessons from Failing. (n.d). Retrieved from https://www.wanderlustworker.com/the-importance-of-failure-5-valuable-lessons-from-failing/

Vance, A. (2015). Elon Musk: Tesla, SpaceX, and the Quest for a Fantastic Future [pdf]. Retrieved from http://1.droppdf.com/files/6CYEX/elon-musk-ashlee-vance.pdf

Winter, C. (2019). 10 Benefits of Reading: Why You Should Read Every Day. Retrieved from https://www.lifehack.org/articles/lifestyle/10-benefits-reading-why-you-should-read-everyday.html